Struggle and Suffrage in Wakefield

Struggle and Suffrage in Wakefield

Women's Lives and the Fight for Equality

Gaynor Haliday

PEN & SWORD
HISTORY
AN IMPRINT OF PEN & SWORD BOOKS LTD.
YORKSHIRE - PHILADELPHIA

First published in Great Britain in 2019 by
Pen & Sword History
An imprint of
Pen & Sword Books Limited
Yorkshire - Philadelphia

ISBN 978 1 52671 7 733

Printed and bound in the UK
by 4edge Ltd, Essex, SS5 4AD

Pen & Sword Books Limited incorporates the imprints of Atlas,
Archaeology, Aviation, Discovery, Family History, Fiction, History, Maritime,
Military, Military Classics, Politics, Select, Transport, True Crime, Air World,
Frontline Publishing, Leo Cooper, Remember When, Seaforth Publishing,
The Praetorian Press, Wharncliffe Local History, Wharncliffe Transport,
Wharncliffe True Crime and White Owl.

For a complete list of Pen & Sword titles please contact
PEN & SWORD BOOKS LIMITED
47 Church Street, Barnsley, South Yorkshire S70 2AS, United Kingdom
E-mail: enquiries@pen-and-sword.co.uk
Website: www.pen-and-sword.co.uk

Or

PEN AND SWORD BOOKS
1950 Lawrence Rd, Havertown, PA 19083, USA
E-mail: Uspen-and-sword@casematepublishers.com
Website: www.penandswordbooks.com

Contents

Foreword

When I began my research for this book, I had only limited notion of the struggles of women to be heard and recognised. What I discovered was our female ancestors were determined that women should be listened to, but knew that women would have to fight to gain the same rights and opportunities as those granted to men.

Over the 100-year period covered by this book, the women of Wakefield acted collaboratively, both locally and nationally, to improve the lives of other women – whether that was in schools, the home, raising children, looking after women's health and well-being, or improving opportunities in the workplace and fighting for better pay and conditions.

Fortunately, much of their work was recorded – in newspapers and minutes of meetings – although much of the written history of Wakefield focuses on the worthy men and the city they built.

The women of Wakefield, whose struggle is recorded in this book, came from many different backgrounds. I have tried to put their work into context with the social and political issues affecting the lives of women nationally at the time. All women are noted by their own first names rather than their husbands' (which is how most married women were recorded).

Thanks to these women's hard work and dedication, women today have opportunities, choices and freedoms that they could only have imagined. I feel saddened that they are no longer here to see what they achieved, but pleased to be able to tell the stories of at least some of the inspiring women of Wakefield.

I would like to thank the following for their help in my research:

Mr Richard Donner and Mr John Donner of The Wakefield Shirt Company, for relating the history of the company and providing images. Mr John Sugden and Mr David Sugden of Wm. Sugdens, Wakefield, for relating their company history and loaning me their family scrapbooks. Mr Geoff Wood, for the story of his aunt, Ida Lessons. Paul L. Dawson for information regarding the Barmby family. Elsie Walton for information about the Pilkingtons of Chevet Hall. Mr Nigel Beaumont for additional information and images of his grandmother, Gwendoline Beaumont.

Elaine Merckx (Wakefield Grammar School Foundation archivist) and Neal Rigby (also WGSF) for images and information about former Wakefield Girls' High School mistresses and pupils. Mrs Hazel Beevers, Ms Denise Green and Mrs Claire Crossdale for family photographs. Mrs Claire McKinlay of St John's Church, for images. Staff at West Yorkshire Archives Service, Wakefield and at Wakefield Local Studies Library for access to records. Wakefield Libraries and Twixt Aire and Calder for images. Wakefield Museums for images.

CHAPTER ONE

Wakefield, an introduction

What was Wakefield like in the 1850s? *William White's Directory* of 1854, in which he created 'an historical sketch and topographical survey for each parish, town, and township, in these great seats of the woollen and worsted manufactures and other parts of the West Riding of Yorkshire', describes Wakefield as 'a large opulent, and handsome market town, pleasantly seated on the north side of the navigable river Calder and the Lancashire and Yorkshire Railway.'

Even though Wakefield was not officially recognised as the county headquarters of the West Riding of Yorkshire until a local government act of 1888, White noted that in many civil matters it was the capital of the West Riding. It held the principal court at the election of Members of Parliament, had a register office for deeds, a prison, an asylum, the office of clerk of the peace, 'and other institutions applicable to the whole Riding'.

Visitors to Wakefield in 1850, entering from the south would have crossed its 'broad and handsome bridge of eight arches', with its Gothic-style chapel, recently restored in 1847. The town extended northwards over the vale of the River Calder and the streets were described as regular, handsome, and spacious, with well-built houses chiefly constructed of brick. Houses, particularly in the suburbs, were large and lofty, and 'beautified with gardens and shrubberies'.

Of course this was not the whole of Wakefield. Off main highways such as Westgate and Kirkgate, hidden behind the homes of landed proprietors, corn merchants and solicitors, lay small yards, such as Stringer's Yard and Salt Pie Alley. These housed the poor, and included widows who worked as charwomen, or had turned to pot-hawking or rag-sorting to make ends meet. Some residents were merely listed as paupers or in receipt of parish relief.

The geographical location of Wakefield, well-linked to other parts of the country via the Aire and Calder, and the Salter and Hebble Navigations, had already established it as a centre for commerce. It held a weekly market every Friday, where corn and wool were traded and provisions could be purchased. Fortnightly cattle fairs had been established since 1765, where even in 1850 there were around 800 'fat cattle' and 6,000 sheep sold every second Wednesday (the largest market in the north) and each year there were two major cattle fairs – in July and November.

The old market place wasn't large and became even less adequate as the population grew. It was attractive, however, with a Doric cross at its centre, open colonnades supporting a dome, and a staircase to a spacious, lantern-lighted room in which public business was transacted. By 1854, a new market place, market house and slaughterhouses had been constructed by the Borough Market Company under the powers of an 1847 Act of Parliament. The right had been given to purchase and clear away many houses and cottages and replace them with spacious and commodious buildings in which to conduct the business of the day. The slaughterhouses were at the top of Goody Bower (just north of the cathedral, east of what is now Brook Street) and 'conveniently arranged'.

At the top of Westgate the elegant Corn Exchange, constructed in 1837, allowed trade to be negotiated indoors. This facility attracted corn merchants to settle in Wakefield – there were twenty-four companies registered, plus seven corn mills. Malting was also big business, with thirty maltsters listed in the directory.

The Tammy Hall in Wood Street, where worsted cloth or 'tammies' had been exhibited and sold since 1777, was in use as a manufactory. It was little used for trade since most of the woollen trade had already migrated to other West Riding towns, particularly Bradford, which, in 1854, had 210 woollen, worsted and yarn spinners compared with Wakefield's twenty-five.

Some local collieries owned direct railways into town and huge quantities of coal could be transported onwards by barge from the wharfs on the Calder eastwards to Gainsborough, Hull and Selby.

Other industries reflected the location and purpose of Wakefield. There were boat-builders, roperies and iron foundries, accountants, agents and auctioneers. Supporting the courts were attorneys, stationers, booksellers and printers. Two newspapers were printed weekly. And for a town that attracted traders from all over the country, more than 100 inns and taverns provided refreshment and accommodation.

For the day-to-day needs of the 48,900 or so residents there were bakers, butchers, tripe-dressers, grocers and tea-dealers; boot- and shoe-makers, milliners, dressmakers and tailors; builders, bricklayers and plumbers.

The Wakefield Union had been created from four townships of Wakefield parish (Wakefield, Alverthorpe with Thornes, Stanley with Wrenthorpe, and Horbury, plus fourteen other townships – East and West Ardsley, West Bretton, Chevet, Crigglestone, Emley, Flockton, Oulton-with-Woodlesford, Shitlington, Sharlstone, Sandal Magna, Walton, Warmfield-cum-Heath, and Thorpe. A Union Workhouse had been built in 1851 in Park Lane, with room for 360 paupers. Only one woman held a senior role in 1851, and she was the matron, Mrs Mary Child, wife of Benjamin Child, the workhouse master. Soon after its opening it was housing forty-two women, thirty-three men and thirty-five children but by 1881 it was full, and matron, Mrs Emma Sophia Jarrard, was assisted by Mary Elizabeth Riley and two nurses, Harriet Baines and Ann Arnold.

The House of Correction, the common gaol of the West Riding, at the bottom of Westgate, had been enlarged in 1821 and again in 1837. A new prison was constructed adjoining the original gaol between 1843 and 1847 and by 1851 was home to around 860 male and 67 female prisoners, and 5 prisoners' daughters. Fifteen women worked here; matrons Jane Shepherd (the governor's mother) Zillah Paige, Sarah Johnson, Mary Whitefield, Mary Flockton and Mary Crossland, and nine servants. Any families of the governors, matrons and warders also lived in, including sixteen young women. At that time, none of the warders were women, although by the census of 1881 there were five women warders and by 1901 this had increased to nine (see Appendix 1). The numbers of women in prison also increased, almost trebling by 1871, reducing to around 123 by 1901.

The extensive West Riding Pauper Lunatic Asylum on East Moor, originally opened in 1818, had been extended three times between 1830 and 1847. It was under the control of the West Riding magistrates, with Dr Charles Caesar Corsellis, resident physician and director, assisted by his wife Caroline, matron over the 450 or so inmates.

Other provision for the poor included three sets of almshouses, in which fifteen poor women and ten poor men resided and were given small weekly stipends to live on.

A Dispensary had been founded in Northgate in 1824, and in 1826 a House of Recovery for fever patients on Westgate Common. Miss Mary Hudson was the House of Recovery's matron, Mrs Crowther its president and Miss Heald as secretary, supported by a committee of women (Mrs Stocks, Mrs Tomlinson, Miss Ambler and Miss Ann Brown) plus two physicians and two surgeons. Generous subscriptions and donations were its main source of income, with annual Yeomanry charity balls held at the Exchange Rooms to raise funds for both institutions, with ladies' tickets costing five shillings and men's at 7s 6d. The proceeds in 1852 had raised £20 18s 6d.[1]

The handsome public buildings in Wood Street, erected by subscription in around 1823, were occupied by a newsroom and subscription library (holding 5,500 books). The mechanics institution also used the building for classes, and the upper floor had been adapted for concerts and 'other public amusements'. Also in Wood Street was a public baths with a music saloon above them. Further entertainment was available at Mr Smedley's theatre in Westgate.

As might be expected in Victorian Britain, religion was important. There were four Churches of England and another under construction. Services were held at the Chantry Chapel on the bridge and there was a Roman Catholic church, which was enlarged in 1852 (possibly to serve the influx of Irish to the town), plus ten dissenting chapels (three Wesleyan, two each for Primitive Methodists and Independents, and one each for Baptists, Unitarians and Quakers), most with schools attached.

Some education was available for the children of the town, although very little, if any, was provided free of charge. According to the 1851 census statistics on education, Wakefield had sixty-seven schools, of which thirty-one were publicly run by charitable organisations. The majority of the children who were on the books attended these schools only irregularly or for short periods of time. In addition were thirty-two Sunday Schools.[2]

The oldest educational establishment was the Free Grammar School, founded in 1591, by a charter of Queen Elizabeth, solely for the education of sons of parishioners. The Greencoat School on Westgate had been founded in 1707. Funded by charity it taught and clothed sixty boys and thirty girls. Newer schools included the Lancasterian on Bond Street, founded in 1813, and attended by about 200 children, the West Riding Proprietary School, St John's, built in 1833 by a company of proprietors, the Wesleyan Training School, Thornhill Street built in 1846, and attended by about 180 children and 120 infants, and the Trinity Church School, opened in 1847 for 100 boys and 70 girls.

Plenty of women worked outside the home – at least ninety followed a trade, others worked alongside their husbands in their businesses. There were professionals such as schoolmistresses and nurses, and of course many were in domestic service, either in private houses or in the institutions of the town.

All positions of authority in the town however, were filled by men. The Wakefield MP was George Sandars, a corn merchant who lived at Alverthorpe Hall. The municipal borough was headed by a mayor, eight aldermen and twenty-four councillors. Mr James Witham was the town clerk, Mr James McDonald the chief constable over a superintendent, three inspectors and nineteen constables, Thomas Shillito, town crier and pinder, and the Wakefield coroner and his deputy were Thomas Lee and Thomas Taylor. Clerk to the Magistrates was Mr J. M. Ianson.

One diligent Wakefield 1851 census enumerator – of the Kirkgate and Wrengate district – perhaps mindful that most women worked in some capacity, allocated every woman in his district some kind of occupation. This is unusual, since most enumerators left the occupation column blank for married women and their daughters, so gives a rare and contemporary insight into what women were really doing. The following is a list of some of the jobs he noted:

- Attends to her family
- Attends to her home
- Keeps a little shop
- Does some gardening
- Hawks caps
- Sells greengrocery and has widow's pay

Even girls were allotted occupations such as 12-year-old Mary Driver who 'attends to her mother' (a widowed pauper) and 13-year-old Hannah Lindley, whose role was to run errands and clean for her grandmother.

More extraordinary were the five women listed as prostitutes, especially William Wainwright's wife, Ellen and their lodger, Jane Block, from Middlesex. Did William know and sanction his wife's work? And was the enumerator being judgemental when he listed prostitutes Ann Walker, Mary Westerman and Jane Frobisher's relationships to the heads of their respective households as 'concubines'? I can find no subsequent trace of either the women or the men with whom they were 'living over the brush', though I had hoped they might have later married.

Wakefield experienced its largest decades of population growth between 1861 and 1871, increasing by twenty-five per cent and again between 1871 and 1881, when the population expanded by almost thirty per cent. Afterwards the population gradually grew by twelve per cent every ten years, although it is difficult to determine exact populations due to boundary changes and inclusions and exclusions of various districts. Still, with birth rates higher than death rates, and a fairly constant stream of people migrating to and from the town, Wakefield, like other towns and cities, continued to grow.

Many of the women of Wakefield, whose work and influence enhanced the lives of other citizens, were not born in the district, but settled here when their husbands or fathers moved into the city for their work. Of course some came independently to pursue jobs – as domestic servants, nurses, matrons or teachers. As women's opportunities widened, so did their mobility in the workplace, so as well as attracting high calibre women to take up professional positions in Wakefield, those born or educated here were also able to follow rewarding careers elsewhere.

One woman, whose long and fruitful life spans almost the whole period covered by this book, was born, raised and died in Wakefield. Edith Grace Mackie was born on 17 January 1853, just eleven months after her father, Robert Bownas Mackie and mother, Fanny Shaw of Stanley Hall, had married at the Zion Chapel on George Street on 4 February 1852. Sadly, Fanny died on 8 May 1853, less than four months after her daughter's birth. Robert, a corn merchant, never remarried. Edith and her father became very close, and she supported him in his many public offices in the town, their family wealth allowing them to subscribe to many good causes. Robert stood for parliament on three occasions, eventually becoming the Liberal MP for Wakefield in 1880. His sudden death in London on 18 June 1885, at the age of 56, caused shockwaves in the town, but it seems Edith was able to carry on his good work for Wakefield. With a substantial inheritance, she was able to live comfortably without need for a career, and had sufficient money to support causes dear to her heart.

One of her first donations was £1,000 to further the restoration work of St John's Church in 1888. This was in addition to the £600 earlier bequeathed to the fund by her father, when she was one of three women invited to lay foundation stones at the base of the new tower. To St John's Home for Girls she was also a most generous subscriber for many years. In 1890, she gave a parcel of land on Balne Lane to be used as a public recreation ground by the children of Wakefield – and as the *Leeds Mercury* reported on 17 February 1890 – spared no trouble or expense in 'rendering the ground wholly suitable for the purpose for which it was to be used and stocking it with requisite gymnastic equipment'. Unfortunately it seems the city council would not later find funds to take over its maintenance as she requested, so Edith took the decision to close it in 1897.

As well as fiscal support to organisations, she gave generously of her time, particularly to St John's Home, where, as a lady visitor, she taught and read to the girls every week. She also held annual parties for them in her own garden and played the piano at fundraising events for the home.

One interesting tale that came to light through some reminiscences of a lady who had worked for Edith from 1937 until Edith's death, was that she had been engaged in her twenties, which would have been in the 1870s. The story, handed down through servants, related how during a grand ball held to celebrate her betrothal, Edith went in search of her 'swain' and found him embracing her cousin, Miss Mary Mackie, behind some potted palms. Not only were they embracing, but Edith overheard the 'swain' telling Mary that although it was she that he truly loved, she was poor and he was only marrying Edith because she was so rich. According to the tale, Edith halted the celebrations, broke off the engagement and sent them both packing. Mary (so the story goes) became a recluse in Scarborough, where she lived with her sister until her death in 1939.

While there might be a fragment of truth somewhere in the story, evidence suggests it might be something concocted by one of Edith's housemaids in a moment of mischief.

Edith didn't have a cousin Mary. She did have some cousins who went to live in Scarborough in the late 1890s, but all were at least sixteen years younger than Edith and well-provided for financially. Of her other cousins (both on her paternal and maternal side) there is only one possible candidate, Annie Gertrude Smith, whose mother (Edith's aunt, Ann Mackie) had married a parson and was living in Suffolk in the 1870s. Could she have been the guilty party? We shall never know.

When she passed away on 19 February 1941, after a short illness, the *Yorkshire Post* commented:

REVERED IN WAKEFIELD Miss Mackie Dies Age 88.

Miss Edith Grace Mackie, the last member of a well-known Wakefield family, died today at her home [Amberd] at Blenheim Road, aged 88. She was the only child of the late Mr Robert Bownas Mackie, MP for Wakefield from 1880 to 1885. To patients at the Wakefield Clayton Hospital Miss Mackie was a constant friend over a long period, visiting the Institution several times a week, and taking an active part in the administration as a member of the governing body. She was one of the founders of the Victoria Nursing Association and St John's Home for Girls claimed large part of her interest, while church organisations, diocesan and parochial, received her generous support. Miss Mackie had lived almost all her life in the St John's district of Wakefield, and was able to attend services at St John's Church until last December. She did not fail seriously in health until few weeks ago.

A true woman of Wakefield.

CHAPTER TWO

Educating and Training Wakefield's Girls

How important was education for girls in 1850? The census return of 1851 shows the UK population of children under 10 years old to be almost equally split between boys and girls. Of the 4,168 children on the books of Wakefield's schools, almost fifty-six per cent were boys. Assuming Wakefield's population ratios were similar to those nationwide, this higher percentage suggests education for boys was slightly more important than for girls. At the time of the census on 31 March 1851 attendance at the 'public' schools was only seventy-five per cent of those registered, compared with ninety-five per cent of those at 'private' schools. This might indicate the parents of those paying more for their children to be educated held school attendance in high regard.

White's Directory of 1854 gives a fairly comprehensive list of academies in Wakefield. The principal grammar school had been founded in 1591, when the citizens of Wakefield, recognising the importance of education, had opened The Grammar School of Queen Elizabeth at Wakefield, 'for the teaching, instructing and bringing up of children and youths in grammar, and other good learning, to continue to that use forever'. It was, and still is, solely for the education of boys. It moved from its location at Goody Bower in 1855, after the West Riding Proprietary School on Northgate, which had been founded in 1834, closed and was put up for sale in November 1854.

Another longstanding school, the Greencoat School, created from a merger of two older schools – the Storie Petty School (founded 1674) and the Charity School (founded prior to 1703) offered education to the poorest boys and girls of the town. Girls were taught separately from boys by 40-year-old Miss Elizabeth Hinchcliffe. According to *White's Directory* of 1837, the children were clothed in green and instructed in reading, writing and arithmetic. Girls were also taught sewing and household work. There was a payment made for children who attended school, perhaps to offset the wages they could have earned and encourage them as scholars instead. The notes also state that in 1837, the master of the boys' school received a salary of £73 10s and the girls' mistress £30 yearly, which perhaps isn't quite as inequal as it seems, since there were twice as many boys as girls to educate. Both teachers had accommodation provided.[3]

The Lancasterian School in Little Bond Street followed a monitorial system introduced by Joseph Lancaster, a Quaker from Southwark. Concerned that poorer classes were denied an education and teachers' salaries were the main cost, he devised a scheme whereby one teacher was assisted by older children (monitors, usually girls) who already had some education. The plan was designed to provide a cheap basic education using limited resources. About 200 boys and 150 girls attended. The Wakefield Lancasterian School must have been quite progressive, as a report in the *Daily Gazette for Middlesbrough*, 8 January 1878, highlighted that for about twenty years it had used such an effective method of teaching infants to read, it was attracting attention from school boards in London and Leeds.

The report related how the children were not taught the names of the letters, but their sounds (phonics). One of their first exercises was to acquire some forty or so different sounds, after which they were gradually brought onto more difficult reading. The system was confined to infant schools, and meant that when children progressed to other schools they were able to 'pick up a book and get on with it at once'. It was opined that a saving of about a year in learning to read was effected.

A Mr Parker, who had seen the work at Wakefield, was struck with the distinctness with which the letters were pronounced and the absence of all provincialisms [accents], even though in Wakefield 'provincialism was very strongly marked'.

In 1854, the headmaster at the Lancasterian School was Mr Benjamin Fox, and his wife Marcy ran the girls' school, assisted by Miss Elizabeth Slater. It is interesting to note that a married woman was teaching, since it later became expected practice for women to give up their careers once wed.

The National Schools were set up by the Church of England, on a similar basis to the Lancasterian model and by 1851 there were 17,000 such elementary schools nationally. Teaching centred on church liturgy and catechism. In Wakefield the boys' school (attended by more than 200 boys) was on Bond Street and the girls' in Almshouse Lane taught around 150 pupils. In 1837 it cost a penny a week for each child to attend school.

Other National Schools in Wakefield, listed in 1854, included St Andrew's, founded in 1845 and Trinity Church School opened in 1847, for 100 boys and 70 girls, which in 1854 was under the tutelage of John Kitchingman and Ann Chadwick. Larger than this was the Wesleyan Training School in Thornhill Street, built in 1846 and attended by 180 children and 120 infants. Elizabeth Long was the infants' mistress, with John A. Long, and Ann Riley named as teachers.

Other public schools listed in *Slater's Directory* of 1855 were infants' schools at Sandal, Quebec Street (founded 1829 and attended by ninety boys and thirty girls), and Thornes, all with a school mistress in charge; village schools at Horbury and Alverthorpe, plus National Schools at Alverthorpe, Horbury and Thornes for older children.

The private schools were sometimes not much more than childcare establishments, where women (often unqualified) taught rudimentary reading and writing in their own homes, charging as much as 4d a week for this service. It is difficult to know how many of these 'Dame Schools' existed in Wakefield, but there were a number of eponymous schools in various parts of the town. These included Miss Ashton and Mrs Beaton's school in Barstow Square, The Misses (M., H. and B.) Healds' school at 102 Northgate (both of which also took boarders) and Mrs Katherine Gawthorpe, also of Northgate, widow of Samuel Thurlstone Wade Gawthorpe, a corn merchant from Liverpool who had settled in Wakefield. She was listed as an annuitant in 1851, and her son and four daughters were listed as 'scholars at home'. Presumably she educated other children too. Some private schools definitely aspired to high standards – Mary Scholes Roach and her sister Elizabeth ran a school and in 1851 described their occupations as 'Young Ladies' Luminary', although this had been changed to 'schoolmistress' by 1861. Martha Irwin and Mary Horrocks also ran a Ladies' School from Rectory House on Warrengate. And again, for another school catering solely for girls, this advertisement appeared in the *Bradford Observer,* 3 January 1850:

> YORK HOUSE, WAKEFIELD.— The Misses JAGGER and JACKSON respectfully announce that their School duties will be resumed on the 25th of January, 1850, when two Ministers' daughters can be received at a reduction from the usual charge.

In many ways Wakefield was no different to other towns at the time. Education for boys seemed more important than for girls, who were expected to marry, be provided for and bring forth the next generation. Accordingly girls were instructed in reading, needlework and other subjects related to homemaking.

Education for all

By the 1860s, matters on education were moving forward nationally. There was a Schools Enquiry Commission (The Taunton Commission), which in 1868 reported there was little secondary education for girls and questioned their ability to learn Latin and maths, plus in 1869, the National Education League started a campaign for free, compulsory and non-religious elementary education for all. Bearing in mind many schools were funded by religious denominations, which sought to keep religious instruction in schools, it met with much resistance from an opposing body – the National Education Union.

Education was also the key topic for other organisations. One notable contributor to the cause, Canon Charles Kingsley, author of *The Water Babies*, spoke passionately about the rights of all to be educated, during the Social Science Congress at Bristol's Victoria Rooms in early October 1869. Declaring the state had a right to compel the ignorant to learn – since those who needed education most, cared for it least – he questioned whether it was really better to make the labouring class pay the school pence for the education of their children or whether it would be wiser to make them pay school rates, similar to the poor rates, and open the schools for free. On the subject of female education, he commented it was women's lack of education that,

> […] leaves to many a fair savage – and many not of our lowest, but lower and middle-class, are nothing else – with no rational or profitable occupation, sense of duty or responsibility, no intellectual exercise (if she can read) save the perusal of illicit and exciting novels; and no ideal life, save one which will give the fullest scope to vanity, luxury, and passion. On behalf of these, the most pitiable of all the victims of ignorance, I urge earnestly on every man and every woman this room, the duty of offering girls some education which will teach them what vast numbers of middle class girls are not now taught, that there are higher objects in life than finery and amusement; that they are responsible to themselves, the State, and to God for the precious gift of womanhood.

> *Bradford Observer*, 2 October 1869

The *Yorkshire Post and Leeds Intelligencer,* 18 December 1869, detailed the heads of a bill prepared by the Executive Committee of the National Education League, to be introduced into Parliament in the session of 1870. The subsequent bill included most of, although not all, their wishes, and the Education Act was introduced on 17 February 1870.

School boards were set up to build and manage new schools where needed, and to oversee the existing voluntary schools. On 17 February 1871, The *Bradford Observer* reported the Wakefield School Board had held its first meeting and elected Mr Edward Green as chairman and Rev. H. Jones as vice chairman.

At the Wakefield board's second meeting on 7 March, a design for a common seal for the board was approved from those put forward. The neat design featured a seated central female figure surrounded by three children whom she was instructing. Around the figures were the words 'Receive instruction that thou mayest be wise' and at the foot 'Wakefield School Board, 1871'. The design had been submitted by Miss Louisa Fennell, who was studying at the Wakefield School of Art. It is interesting that the chosen design was of a female figure, since it symbolised the importance of women as educators – also emphasised by the 1870 Act permitting female householders to vote and stand for office on school boards (although Wakefield's board was made up entirely of men).

Its third meeting, in April, saw the Wakefield School Board officially adopt the principle of compulsory education and in May, as required by the Act, the returns of children in attendance at the various schools within the borough were presented and discussed. This was to ascertain whether there was a shortfall in provision of school places. The number of scholars on the books of all schools in the district was 4,724. The registrar's figures showed there were 2,440 children aged between 3 and 5, who would be coming up to the school starting age, and 4,200 between 5 and 13 years old. With existing school accommodation available for 7,693 children, there seemed no urgency to build new Board Schools. However, standards in some existing schools (now under more scrutiny) needed to improve, and in July one member of the board urged that steps to improve the efficiency of the Greencoat School should be taken. This might have tied in with the board's letter to Her Majesty's Inspector of Schools, enquiring when he intended to pay his proposed visit to Wakefield.

After much discussion and negotiation, the first Board School in Wakefield was built at the bottom of Westgate in 1874. An advert in the *Yorkshire Post and Leeds Intelligencer*, 15 May 1874, revealed it would open after the midsummer holidays and invited applications for experienced teachers for this mixed and infants' school. A master was required for the mixed school of 164 children at a salary of £140, and a mistress for the 373 infants – at a salary of £75 (note the disparity in wages and responsibilities), plus an assistant mistress to teach in the infants' department and to act as sewing mistress for girls in the mixed school. A certified teacher would receive £65 salary, but an ex-pupil teacher only £40. Pupil teachers were those who underwent a four-year training period prior to taking their certificate examinations. There were fifty-five applicants for the master's position and nine for the office of mistress. Mr Henry Samuel Goodyear and his wife Mary (both with six years' experience in charge of a Sheffield school) were appointed as master and mistress and the assistant's role went to 19-year-old Miss Martha Ann Rhodes, previously engaged as a pupil teacher at the Lancasterian School. Her salary was £40, although all salaries were to be reviewed annually and hers would certainly increase on qualification. Martha later went on to be the infants' mistress at Eastmoor Board School.

The school opened on 3 August 1874, with accommodation for about 440 children. The total cost of creating this new school had been almost £4,000, and it was reported that an efficient staff of teachers had been engaged and around 150 scholars attended on the first day, more than had been anticipated, since the fees were 'quite as high as those of the best elementary schools of the town'.

Yet prior to education being made compulsory for children up to 10 years old by the Elementary Education Act of August 1880, not all parents sent their children to school regularly. Despite the entreaties of the National Education League there were fees to pay (except for the poorest, whose fees were paid by the school board), and children could be usefully employed in the home. One headmaster of a West Riding school noted (with some frustration) in his school logbook that a number of girls had been kept at home to help nurse siblings and fetch water. He was particularly irritated when attendance was low in December 1872, because they were 'doing paltry jobs for their mothers who say they are cleaning down for Christmas' and added: 'I find the parents who are always grumbling as to the progress of their children are the very people who invariably keep them at home to do such petty jobs.'

In February 1881, the Wakefield School Board's annual report showed there were 6,071 school places in the borough and 128 teachers. The number of children on the books exceeded the places available by 753, but average attendance in 1880 had been 3,773, still only fifty-five per cent.

Secondary education for girls

As elementary education became accessible to all, the governors of Wakefield Free Grammar of Queen Elizabeth, heeding the Endowed Schools Act of 1869, founded the Wakefield Grammar School Foundation in 1875. Its aim was to provide (in a separate school from the boys) secondary education up to university entrance for girls, using endowments that had been previously used exclusively for boys' education.

The *Sheffield Daily Telegraph*, 24 January 1878 reported:

WAKEFIELD ENDOWED HIGH SCHOOL FOR GIRLS. A short time ago a new scheme was framed by the Endowed Schools Commissioners, which gave permission to the governors of the charities at Wakefield to establish in that town a high school for girls. For some time past the governors have been taking steps to carry out this part of the scheme, and to provide a first-class school in the town for young ladies. [...]

[...] Having re-organised the boys' school, the governors turned their attention to the high school for girls, and it will shortly be opened. It was intended to erect a new building for the school, but whilst that project was under consideration Mr Elias Holt, of Wentworth House, offered to dispose of his residence to the governors for the purpose of being utilised as the new school, and the mansion, which is probably the best in the town, and is situate near St John's, the most fashionable part of the borough, was purchased for £8,000. Yesterday, a meeting of the governors was held at their offices in Market Street for the purpose of electing a lady to act as headmistress of the new school. The salary offered was very liberal, being £2 per head per year for each pupil in the school, besides a fixed salary of £100 per year, and apartments in the school. The applications were sent in by the 1st inst., and it was then found that there were 34 candidates for the post. That number was gradually reduced, and at the meeting yesterday five candidates were in attendance. At the close of a long sitting, over which the Rev. W. M. Madden, spokesman, presided, Ellen Allen, of Newnham College, Cambridge, was appointed to take charge of the school.

The salary was half the pay of the headmaster of the boys' school, which was £200 per year, plus £4 per head.

Provision was made to educate 100 girls and advertisements were placed in newspapers as follows:

WAKEFIELD ENDOWED HIGH SCHOOL FOR GIRLS, WENTWORTH HOUSE. The School will open September 16th, 1878. Head Mistress: MISS ALLEN. Certificated Cambridge Student, Clothworker's Scholar, Newnham Hall, Cambridge. Assistant Mistresses: MISS WILKINSON, 1st Class Cambridge Certificate. MISS DAGG. 1st Class Cambridge Certificate. MISS BRITTAIN. Bedford College, London. The prospectus may be obtained, with form of application for admission of scholars into the School, from the Clerk to the Governors, Market Street, Wakefield.

Although these teachers were educated to degree level their qualifications were documented as university certificates, since Cambridge University did not permit women to use the title of degree until 1921.

To gain entry to the school, girls had to pass an entrance exam. Fees were £10 per school year. The first intake was of fifty-eight girls aged between 8 and 17 years, who generally had academic lessons in the morning and instruction in music, sewing and drawing in the afternoon. The headmistress and staff lived on the upper floors of Wentworth House.

Six months later an advertisement appeared in the *Yorkshire Post and Leeds Intelligencer* advising:

> A house in connection with the WAKEFIELD ENDOWED HIGH SCHOOL FOR GIRLS was opened on the 21st April by Miss EMILY WILKINSON for the reception of pupils from a distance.

Emily was the sister of Miss Wilkinson, the assistant mistress, and ran a kindergarten and prep school at the premises at Coverham House, Middle Row, St John's, Wakefield. The house was described as being near the school, with a field behind it for recreation. Termly fees for board and residence were £12 5*s* for full boarders and £8 15*s* for weekly.

By 1879 there were 110 girls learning English literature and grammar, arithmetic, algebra, history, geography, French, German, Holy Scripture and Euclid.

However, the fees of £10 a year put girls' secondary education out of reach of most families and there was some discord from those who saw the school as somewhere for only the wealthy. This was quickly addressed in 1882, by a scheme providing scholarships for girls from the public elementary schools to attend on reduced fees. There were twenty-nine applicants for the ten places, and thanks to additional funding from Richard Holdsworth JP of Sandal, the scholarships provided completely free education. By 1897, the provision of scholarships was through the council and there were twenty-eight places offered.

One of the first scholarship girls was Louisa Chadwick, whose father, Walter, was a maltster's clerk. The family lived at Regent Street, Sandal. Louisa left school in 1885, aged 17, to train at Whitelands Training College in Roehampton, a teacher training college for women. Her training completed, she returned to the family in Sandal and took a teaching post at Sandal CE Infants, eventually becoming headmistress. One of her sisters, Kate, became a sewing mistress, another a milliner and the third a dressmaker and costumier.

The Cambridge University exams were a very important part of school life, with an external examiner visiting the school and publishing his report in the newspapers. By the 1890s there were a number of girls going to university – mainly to Newnham and Girton at Cambridge, but also some of the northern universities. Many of these well-educated girls never married, enjoying the financial independence of good careers as teachers, headmistresses, doctors, midwives.

As numbers grew, so did the range of subjects. By 1898, girls were being taught physics and chemistry, using the laboratory at the newly opened technical college to conduct experiments until the school installed its own chemistry laboratory in 1905. The very popular domestic science lessons started in 1903, and in 1905 Greek was added to the curriculum. By 1916, the school was also offering secretarial courses in shorthand and typing.

New secondary school regulations issued by the Board of Education in 1917, saw the introduction of a School Certificate for girls leaving at 16 and a Higher School Certificate for those who stayed a further two years for higher work and probably university. This was continued until the introduction of GCEs in 1951.

Secondary education for Wakefield's girls became more accessible when the council bought Thornes Park estate in 1919. The original plan was to convert Thornes House and twenty acres of the estate to create a school and use the remaining ninety-two acres for council housing. Only the school was accepted by the housing commission, and Thornes House School was founded in 1921, with separate secondary education for girls and boys. The first headmistress of Thornes Girls' School was Winifred Grace Chinneck (Manchester) BA, with Miss Le Mare as her deputy.

By 1928 it was reported the Thornes House secondary schools were steadily making a fine tradition and gradually taking their place among the secondary schools of the country as they aimed for distinction. Eight boys passed the Higher School Certificate that year, three more than previously, and five girls were successful in the first time in the history of the school, with Mary Johnson obtaining the full certificate and Nancy Cooke obtaining a scholarship to study at Liverpool University.[4] The school and girls continued to progress and in the 1930s the school had 230 girls, taught by ten mistresses, each qualified in specialist subjects. In 1941 the school became co-ed and it became a Grammar School in 1944 under the new Education Act.[5]

A House of Refuge and Reform

One of the concerns brought up by the National Education League was that children who had no education had limited job prospects and possibly limited morals. At a meeting in Leeds on 29 November 1869, (*Yorkshire Post and Leeds Intelligencer*, 30 November 1869) the mayor of Leeds, who chaired the meeting and had been on the first educational committee of the city thirty years earlier, stated the present system of education did little for those who needed it most. Even after thirty years of government grants to voluntary schools, those who were with the greatest ignorance had received nothing at all, the streets were swarming with children needing education – and these were thieves, tramps and vagrants. The mayor remarked that even the Ragged Schools, specifically founded for the lowest class of children, did not admit these children 'if they could help it', and one particular school, with a capacity of 120 children had seen 400 children attend in a year – meaning they only averaged four months of schooling. Little wonder some children fell into a life of crime and ended up in gaol.

Even women and girls who found themselves on the wrong side of the law, often for petty crimes, faced spells in gaol. Without a social services structure to help them become useful members of society many fell back into their old habits after serving their sentences. With a large gaol in the vicinity, these women would have been a visible presence on Wakefield's streets.

At the instigation of a Mrs Hamer, Wakefield established a Refuge for Discharged Female Prisoners in 1848 at St John's. The *Leeds Intelligencer*, reporting on the West Riding Spring Quarter Sessions on 3 April 1848, in Pontefract stated:

> The proposition for House of Refuge, at Wakefield, for discharged female prisoners and boys, brought before the court by the Rev. J. A. Rhodes, is well worthy of general attention. The proposed institution has been originated by a benevolent and philanthropic lady (Mrs Hamer of Wakefield), and is to be supported by voluntary contributions. We hope that her endeavours to rescue, as it were, 'the brand from the burning' will be liberally seconded by the public.

The establishment opened on 10 July 1848, and the *Leeds Intelligencer*, 28 October 1848 added:

> [The] House of Refuge at Wakefield, for females discharged from prison, is approved of, as likely to be beneficial to the parties for which it is intended, and highly useful to the West Riding of Yorkshire. The description of persons for whom this benevolent institution is principally intended are of all objects undoubtedly the most pitiable. It is well ascertained that many young females, whose evil course in life has brought them within the precincts of a prison, have a sincere desire on being discharged to become honest and useful members of society, but are irresistibly driven to their old haunts of vice, and soon relapse into their former habits, from the impossibility of procuring honest employment. Discarded by their friends, despised by too

many—shut out from all legitimate intercourse with the society of the good and virtuous, there is no hope,— the 'Father's house to which the prodigal can return', is closed against them irrevocably; can we then wonder the result when the dreadful alternative is destitution and misery and premature death?

[...] The establishment of a Refuge at Wakefield, in the immediate vicinity of one of our largest prisons, is obviously well worthy of approval, in reference to the locality chosen. Its doors will be nigh, to invite within its asylum the forlorn creatures who, having expiated their offences against the laws of their country in the durance of the gaol, where, haply [sic], a wholesome moral and religious discipline has excited in them sorrow for their past errors and a yearning for the duties and privileges of virtuous life, are, but for such a refuge as this, destitute of everything except the opportunity—(by the pressure of want, almost the necessity)—of returning to their former haunts and evil courses. This House of Refuge is intended to admit, not only females, but also youths of the other sex, discharged from prison, a class equally with the other capable of being reclaimed, or liable to be destroyed, by circumstances. No nobler work of benevolence can demand our sympathy. Reformed prison discipline may correct the heart, but what revives the blighted reputation? Here charity is called upon and the call will not be despised. This work, the dictates of a benevolent and generous female heart have suggested, and in which she has, as an example worthy of her sex, taken the initiative, will not, we are persuaded, languish for the means needful for its successful prosecution. The names of the subscribers already obtained, including many of the magistracy of the Riding, are a guarantee to assure us of this expectation. [...]

In February 1849, the managers of the House of Refuge presented their first report to the magistrates, stating:

[They] feel great pleasure in stating that the object for which the institution was opened has hitherto given them every hope of its ultimate benefit. They have at the same time some reluctance, at so early a period of the establishment, in giving a decided opinion of the good that has hitherto been effected, but have great faith in casting bread upon the waters, knowing 'that it will be found after days hence'. The establishment was opened on the 10th of July, 1848, since which period eleven persons have been admitted. One has been restored to her friends. One has been discharged, being pregnant, consequently not a proper person for the institution. One has been provided with a situation in a respectable family. Seven are now inmates in the institution. Several more are willing to enter as soon as their imprisonment ceases. The managers beg to state, as the inmates of the establishment were, previous to their admission, given to understand that it was a voluntary act on their part to become inmates, two only have been disappointed in their expectations [...]

Leeds Intelligencer, 24 February 1849

Although the refuge was open to boys, there is no evidence of any being admitted. The 1851 census reveals that Mrs Fanny Hesling (née Bailey, in Ripon) was the matron at the home. Aged only 26 and with a 2-year-old daughter and month-old son and living apart from husband John, whom she'd married in 1848, it must have been a tough job. A visitor to the home was Bessy Bailey, matron at Manchester Gaol, who appears to be her older sister. Fanny was assisted by two general servants, Mary Ann Seaburn and Priscilla Armitage. The eighteen girls, listed as inmates, were aged between 12 and 25. As Wakefield gaol received prisoners from all parts of the country, not all were local lasses.

Two Acts of Parliament were passed in the 1850s to deal with the issues of young offenders. The first, in 1854, was the

Youthful Offenders Act, which stated that any child convicted of an offence could be sentenced to a short spell in prison, followed by a period of two to five years in a Reformatory School. It also enabled voluntary reformatories to be approved by the Inspector of Prisons. To provide space for a reformatory, part of Wakefield's House of Refuge was converted to accommodate girls in October 1856.

The second Act, The Industrial School Act 1857, empowered magistrates to sentence children between the ages of 7 and 14 to a period in a Reformatory or Industrial School. It included children brought before court for vagrancy or homelessness. There was a distinction between Industrial and Reformatory schools, in that the former received the destitute, whereas the latter were reserved for juvenile offenders, many of whom had been before the courts more than once.

A further act was passed in 1861 to include children apparently under the age of 14, begging or receiving alms, or found wandering without any means of support or a home, or in the company of thieves. Children under 12 could be sent to a reformatory school (rather than prison) for committing punishable offences. And if parents of a child under the age of 14 declared her to be beyond their control, they could send her to the reformatory.

Wakefield's House of Refuge (with the name in full of the Refuge and Reformatory School) continued its work, taking both discharged female prisoners and girls committed to the Reformatory.

Records from the Register of Wakefield Reformatory School 1856–65 show the youngest inmate to be 7-year-old Ann Elizabeth Lee, born in Rastrick in 1852 and admitted to the institution on 16 August 1859. On 7 June 1859 she had been sentenced to two months' imprisonment and five years in a Reformatory by magistrates at Sheffield Petty Sessions, for the offence of being a rogue and a vagabond. Her residence at the time of her offence was in Sheffield with her father, a steel worker. The notes state that she had no education and had been harshly treated by her parents. She was removed to a new Reformatory in Doncaster in September 1861.

The census of 1861 shows 30-year-old Miss Nancy Nicholson from Mayo, Ireland as the superintendent of the Reformatory, assisted by Martha Tyas, whose title was schoolmistress, Annie Driffield, sewing mistress and Margaret Ann Sherwood, laundress. As further indication that this was a place of training and education, all the other girls were listed as scholars rather than inmates. By this time the refuge and reformatory had expanded and there were forty-three females, the youngest being Ann Lee (as above) and the eldest, Mary Dawson, aged 36.

Margaret Ann Sherwood had been sentenced to the Reformatory for a four-year spell on 17 March 1857, after a month's imprisonment for stealing boots. She was 12 years old. She had had four years' education, could read a little and was described as sharp and intelligent-looking. Good behaviour earned her a job within the institution and she became housemaid in May 1859, then laundress, before being transferred to Doncaster in 1861.

After Margaret's departure, Fanny Maria Driffield took over as laundress. Fanny Maria was Annie Driffield's sister and had spent twelve months in Lincoln Gaol for larceny at a dwelling-house in 1858. As a discharged female prisoner she is not on the Reformatory records, nor is Annie. Fanny met with a tragic death at the refuge in January 1861. The *Barnsley Chronicle*, 5 January 1861, ran the report under the headline of 'MELANCHOLY OCCURRENCE AT THE WAKEFIELD REFORMATORY,' telling how Fanny had died as a result of fumes from a coal-burning stove in the bedroom she shared with Mary Anne Barnes. Mary had woken to the sound of Fanny making noise in her throat, and had tried to fetch her a drink of water, but had fallen unconscious herself. When the girls did not turn up for duty in the morning, and other inmates couldn't rouse them (the door being locked) Miss Nancy Nicholson was sent for. Fanny was lying on her bed, struggling to breathe and Mary was face down on the floor, quite insensible. A doctor tried to pump the girls' stomachs, which apparently worked with Mary, but Fanny was so comatose her epiglottis had closed and the tube went into the windpipe instead. They tried to administer ammonia and brandy, and when she failed to swallow more than a few drops, proceeded with a turpentine enema. Poor Fanny remained comatose until she passed away the next morning. A post-mortem revealed all her internal organs to be congested, a result of suffocation – but also traces of a narcotic, which may have explained why she died while her roommate survived. Her sister Annie stated at the inquest that she did not think her sister suicidal, but pointed a finger of blame on a Sarah Holdsworth who did not get on with Fanny and who'd declined to go and help in the night when her roommate had heard the commotion, saying she was afraid.

Ultimately, the jury agreed the cause of death was from inhaling carbonic acid gas and recommended the stove be removed from the room, and some better means of communication between the matron and the inmates introduced.

In May 1861, after making a full recovery, Liverpool-born Mary Anne Barnes was appointed laundress. Mary had been committed for five years in June 1857, after a thirty-seven day imprisonment for frequently robbing and abusing her mother. She had been transferred to Wakefield from Toxteth to be as far away as possible from the bad characters with whom she had been keeping company. Her notes show she had never quite left home, but was prone to walking out at night in the neighbourhood of the sailors' home. Described as a great liar, she had apparently taken pleasure in the distress caused to her mother in telling her that her son (Mary's brother) had died at sea. Her 'career' in the Reformatory started badly. She was quarrelsome and possessed a 'masterful temper', but gradually settled into life. Her appointment as laundress was short-lived however. Although she did the work itself well, she did not have sufficient control over other girls working alongside her and in August was sent out into service with Mr Roberts, a Wakefield draper. She was returned to the refuge on 4 November – being inclined to be 'unsteady'. Her time expired in January 1862 but, disinclined to return to her widowed mother who could not support her, was allowed to remain as a 'refuge woman'.

Fifteen-year-old twin girls Mary Ann and Elizabeth Yarker from Harrogate, admitted to the Reformatory for a three-year period following their theft of gingerbread, fared rather better once their time in custody was over. Neither had been convicted previously and there is a sense that their crime may have been a childish stunt. Perhaps Elizabeth (described as of good character) was urged on by Mary Ann (who was a 'troublesome, mischief-maker, but improving'), but by 1871 both were earning their own livings as weavers.

One difficulty experienced by the refuge was through trying to carry out two kinds of work that did not necessarily coexist well: discharged women prisoners were free to come and go, while the girls in the Reformatory class were under restraint. To simplify matters it was decided in 1865 to transfer the Reformatory girls to the new facility in Doncaster. The home changed its name to the West Riding Industrial Home for Discharged Female Prisoners, but received no further government grants, meaning the work had to be supported by voluntary efforts.

Arts and Technology

In complete contrast to the educational work of the Reformatory was the Wakefield School of Art, which opened in Bell Street on 30 March 1868. Proposing to be not merely a school of art, but of science also, and with an art gallery and museum attached to supplement study, it was the first institution of its kind in the country. The school was closely connected to the South Kensington Museum, which sent more than 1,000 items from its collections for the use of pupils. A meeting was held on 28 April to formally open the institution and was attended by various MPs and local dignitaries, all men.

The creation of the Wakefield Industrial and Fine Art Institution, as it was known, had been made possible through profits of £3,000, raised from an Industrial and Fine Art Exhibition in 1865, which had attracted 189,000 visitors in forty days.

As well as a day school attended by thirty pupils, there were night classes for around seventy to eighty students. Scholars travelled from Batley, Horbury, Ossett and Normanton, as well as the Wakefield neighbourhood.

By the seventh annual meeting of the institution, held at the Mechanics' Institute in October 1874, the institution was flourishing, the number of students had increased, classes were well-attended and examination results very satisfactory. There were calls to extend the institution, as science classes were already having to be held elsewhere, and it was proposed to appeal to the inhabitants of Wakefield for help, expecting such an appeal to be met with a hearty response.
The secretary's report stated:

> The School of Art may now be looked upon as one of the most successful educational agencies of the town. During the past year 140 students have attended its classes, being a considerable increase over the number in any previous year. The average time during which individual students remain at the school is becoming longer, and the range of studies now extended to more numerous and more advanced stages of art education. These facts the council regard as conclusive evidence that there is a rapidly growing sense of the value and necessity of art education (particularly among those classes for whose more especial benefit the School of Art was established), and that the advantages offered by it, under the able conduct of the present headmaster, are increasingly appreciated by those who have availed themselves of them.

Addressing the meeting, Mr Sanderson, MP, apologised for his previous neglect to take an interest in the institution and expressed his pleasure in seeing such an array of talent exhibited – especially since so many of the successful students were sons and daughters of some of his old schoolfellows.

Of the hundred prizes presented in various classes, twenty-one went to girls. Annie E. Roxby, daughter of a gas-fitter, who had won a bronze medal and two guineas the previous year, was awarded a National Book prize, a free studentship and a local prize. Her younger sister, Emily, also won a local prize. Annie's occupation in the 1871 census was a dressmaker, so she was probably gaining her education and improving her craft at night classes. It is also likely she met her husband at these classes, as in 1875 she married photographer, Henry Hall, another of the 1874 prize-winners.

Two of the girls who used their training to make a career had both lost their fathers at an early age.

Georgiana Mary Green, born in 1848, was the daughter of George Green, a wine merchant, who died before she was 12 years old. In 1871 she had no occupation, nor was she a scholar, yet in 1874 she gained two awards at the art school and by 1881, aged 32, her occupation was noted as 'artist, painter'.

Susanna Parker Williamson, born 1858, whose father William was chief clerk to the probate registry in Wakefield up until his death in November 1867, aged 45, was a day scholar at the art school. Her education gave her the opportunity to become a governess in Salford, and by 1891 she was teaching music.

Other girls seem to have come from less humble backgrounds, where it appears education for girls was encouraged, or at least there was more money available to pay to educate daughters. Daughters of wine or corn merchants, who went on to marry well, never using their training to pursue a career.

One of the first pupils to train at the art school was the aforementioned Louisa Fennell, who started as soon as it opened. At prizegiving in October 1869, she was awarded top honours for her watercolour painting. Both she and her sister Emily also gained awards for model-drawing and freehand. It wasn't until the census of 1901 that Louisa's occupation was recorded as a watercolour artist, although she had been recognised as such for many years, exhibiting her work as far afield as Penzance. Louisa had six sisters and three brothers, and as the offspring of a wealthy and long-lived wine merchant who passed the business on to his sons, the females seem to have no need to work and only one, Elizabeth, married. One who did strike out into the world of work was Mary Beatrice, who became a matron in Hove, Sussex. Whether there was a family rift it is difficult to know, but her other sisters lived together at 21 St John's Square till their deaths. None left Mary Beatrice any money in their wills, but she outlived them all, dying in Lowestoft in 1953, aged almost 92.

The Wakefield Industrial and Fine Art School continued to play an important role in the education of Wakefield's young people, in 1891 becoming the technical college, when a new building on the same Bell Street site was ceremoniously opened by the Duke of Clarence. The chairman of the school's council declared its work of technical instruction would put within the reach of every working lad in the town the means to make him a fit and skilled artisan, but there was no mention of educating working lasses for commerce and industry. However, in later recognition of the direct value of technical education in meeting the needs of girls, as well as boys, who (it was said) were better suited to vocational rather than academic subjects, it was extended several times in the 1930s, as education in the city underwent changes.

In 1936, further proposals were put forward to meet the needs of a population catchment of 211,500. By this time the art department had been squeezed into the top floor and an outbuilding at the technical college. As many as three classes were sometimes taught in one room and cake decoration classes were held in the printing room. The estimated cost for new art school premises, to be built opposite the Registry of Deeds in Newstead Road, would cost around £40,000, but would cater for 1,000 students from places as far away as Hemsworth, Castleford and Knottingley. It was also noted the technical college had little or no provision for women's work, and more facilities should be provided. The plans were approved in September 1938, but before budgets or work could be fully authorised, war broke out.

During the war, the technical college turned its attention to offering additional courses for service personnel, including special classes in technical and commercial subjects, languages, practical crafts and physical education. The passing of the National Service Act in December 1941, meant unmarried women between 20 and 30 years old were called up to join the auxiliary services – such as the ATS (Auxiliary Territorial Service), WRNS (Women's Royal Naval Service) and WAAF (Women's Auxiliary Air Force). Early in 1944, it was reported that half those who had attended the classes in Wakefield had been girls serving with the ATS. Although many women in the ATS took on support tasks, operating telephones and radars, or working with anti-aircraft gun crews, the special full-time courses arranged for almost 400 ATS members at Wakefield, merely covered a wide range of domestic science subjects. A fortnight's tuition had been given in cookery, make-do-and-mend and minor household repairs. The courses were started on the recommendation of the educational directorate of the ATS, and it was noted that 'as far as those held in Yorkshire are concerned, the experiment has been fully justified'.

An ATS 'School for Brides' was established at Pontefract ATS barracks, with weekly lessons given at Wakefield Technical College. Among the pupils mentioned in the *Yorkshire Post and Leeds Intelligencer,* 4 May 1944, was Private Lena Carver of Cullingworth, who was engaged to a Birmingham man serving in the navy. It seems with little further ambition than to be a homemaker she declared, 'I want my own home, preferably in the country, but near enough to the shops. Of course I want children, three would be best.'

As the war was drawing to an end in April 1945, a homecraft course was initiated at the college. Described as an ambitious scheme to equip Northern Command ATS girls to meet peacetime conditions, about fifty girls 'specially picked for their intelligence and popularity', were to learn everything about homecraft. At the end of five weeks' training they were to return to their units and act as instructors to other girls. It was envisaged that most of the thirty-three hours a week would be devoted to practical work and as an example of an assignment the *Yorkshire Post and Leeds Intelligencer* detailed:

Do the daily work between 8.30 a.m. and 1 p.m. in a household consisting of a husband, wife and two guests. Prepare coffee at 10.30 a.m. Shop and cook for a light lunch for the husband. The wife and guests have been invited lunch at friend's house. Before the week is out they will have to solve such problems as catering for two guests when both wife and husband are working all day. Washing, cleaning, household decoration and repairs, renovating furniture, feeding small children, planning budgets, elementary knowledge of infectious diseases, preserving fruit and knowing how the town or city council operates are all dealt with in this course.

Although it seems girls were thought of as little more than homemakers and expected to return to domestic duties after the war, change was happening. A new part-time training course for Youth Leadership was advertised, organised by the West Riding Association Girls' and Mixed Clubs. It was due to start in September 1945, and would consist of practical experience, visits of observation, reading, written work and discussion, and lectures one night weekly at Wakefield Technical College. Application forms were available from Miss Hazlehurst at the college.

Other women making their mark at the college were Miss Edith Mary Martin (born 1905 and listed on the 1939 Register as teacher at technical college) and Miss Marion Stuart Temple (born 1887 and in 1939 a secondary school teacher), who were assisting men who had lost arms during the war, to learn to type. By revising the standard fingering method (first for a man who had lost his left arm, then again for one who had lost his right) the men were able to graduate at a respectable twenty-five words per minute. Miss Martin, who had remained a spinster, finally found love after George N. Blair, the college principal, was widowed in 1956. Edith and George (who lived next-door-but-one to each other in Wentworth Street) were married in 1958.

Marguerite Moorcroft, invalided out of the WAAF as a 'nervous wreck', was another former war veteran undergoing training and rehabilitation at the college. The only girl in a book-keeping class, she qualified for a job at the GPO bank.

And finally, one woman's career that had gone on hold for 'the duration' won a national competition, promoted by the Design and Research Centre for the Gold, Silver, Silversmiths and Jewellers' Industries to discover new talent in jewellery and silverware designing. Thelma Stanley from Normanton, who had studied at the Wakefield Art School before winning a scholarship to the Royal College of Art in London, had to postpone her studies while she served with the NAAFI. In her final year of study, in 1948, her winning design – of a set of fine jewellery comprising double-clip earrings and necklace in sapphire and diamonds set in platinum – was filmed for television and exhibited at the British Industries Fair in May that year.

CHAPTER THREE

The Working Lives of Wakefield's Ordinary Women

As well as the colourful picture painted by the diligent enumerator in 1851, an insight into the working lives of Wakefield's women may be gained from a study of various trade directories. For example, *Slater's Commercial Directory* of 1855,[6] which lists institutions, occupations and tradespeople, reveals women were engaged in a wide variety of employment. As might be expected there were a fair number of shopkeepers, grocers and dealers, as well as traditional women's jobs as dressmakers, milliners and straw bonnet makers, but it is interesting to note that in a time of growing intemperance, seventeen of Wakefield's public houses had women in charge. Some who'd worked alongside spouses continued to work as publicans after being widowed – Esther Brotherton managed the Old King's Arms in Kirkgate with John until his death in early 1851, then transferred to the nearby Spotted Dog. Mary Ann Anderson was running the Elephant and Castle in Westgate with husband John in 1841, and was still the landlady in 1861, many years after being widowed. Others, such as Ann Spawforth, widow of butcher James, embarked on her own career after his death, taking charge of the Dog Inn, Westgate. None of the women were young and one might imagine them as forthright, down-to-earth, and not easily intimidated by drunken behaviour. The women of Wakefield weren't afraid to tackle other tough jobs either. Sarah Binns of Westgate

Common was a bricklayer and builder, Ann Crawshaw was a currier and leather seller in Kirkgate, Ann Backhouse, also of Kirkgate, was a glazier, plumber and gas fitter. Also keeping a business running after her husband Amos's death was Mary Shires, who carried on as a butcher in Wakefield's Shambles for at least twenty years after being widowed in 1851.

Although women were clearly able and willing to work for a living, an analysis of the occupation data for 1861, shows only thirty-five per cent of women over the age of 20 were in paid employment in Wakefield, compared with forty-eight per cent of similar women in the neighbouring West Riding town of Bradford. Perhaps opportunities for women with little education were limited in Wakefield. After all, twenty-six per cent of the female workforce in Bradford earned wages in its booming textile mills, compared with only 3.4 per cent in Wakefield. Alternatively, Wakefield's men may have been wealthier, meaning there was less need for their womenfolk to earn an income outside the home. This might be suggested by the higher proportion of women (often from outside the district) in domestic service, who came to work in the large homes of Wakefield's upper-middle class families. That there was also money available to pay for education is underlined by the higher proportion (almost double that of Bradford) of teachers and governesses in Wakefield.

Around fifty-four per cent of the age-group were recorded as [non-working] wives and a further four per cent were identified as wives, daughters, granddaughters and so on, of butchers, farmers, publicans, and shopkeepers etc. – in short, women who worked but probably received no pay.

In 1861, by far the largest proportion (ten per cent) of Wakefield's women in paid employment worked in some kind of domestic service, whether in private homes and public institutions, or in tasks such as charring, laundry work or gardening. Other significant employment opportunities were in clothes-making – dressmaking, tailoring, millinery or shoe manufacture. Many of the women thus employed worked from home in their own businesses. Other occupations for women included selling foods of all descriptions – from shops and barrows – keeping lodging houses and coffee shops, or nursing. There were five bookbinders, three beggars or vagrants, two gypsies, three artificial flower makers, two brush makers and a French polisher. And as might be expected for a town with a gaol that incarcerated women, seven women were employed to keep them under control. Also included in the returns (as occupations) were the 304 'lunatics, no stated occupation', and the 44 'prisoners, no stated occupation' (although the enumerator's report shows there were actually 111 female prisoners over the age of 20 and a further 35 aged between 12 and 19).

It is impossible to determine from census returns exactly how many of the working women were employed in factories, nor the functions they carried out. It is likely there was little job mobility, since wages in factories in the town were standardised across industries, perhaps to deter trained employees from moving to rival companies. However, a report in the *Todmorden Advertiser and Hebden Bridge Newsletter,* 19 August 1871, shows the Wakefield factory girls were not afraid to ask for more money for their labours.

STRIKE OF FACTORY GIRLS AT WAKEFIELD.

Up to a fortnight ago all the worsted spinners in Wakefield paid their factory girls 1s 2d per day, or 7 shillings per week. Last Friday fortnight, Messrs G. Lee & Sons gave their girls an advance of 6d per week, and several other manufacturers gave a similar advance. Finding that they had obtained an advance without much difficulty and knowing that at present all the worsted manufacturers were very busy, the girls applied for another advance of 6d per week. On this being refused they struck work, and on Saturday and Monday paraded the streets of the town, singing hymns and songs.

Whether their strike was successful is not recorded.

∞

Many of Wakefield's female heads of households were listed as gentlewomen, independents and annuitants. They were generally widows, sisters, or daughters of men who provided for them financially.

With domestic help taking care of household chores, gentlewomen such as these had little to occupy their time. Rather than pursue leisure pursuits, they used the education that had been afforded them and took an active interest in the welfare and support of others, in charitable, voluntary work. Two early examples are Mrs Sophia Crowther and Mary Pilkington.

Sophia Crowther was the widow of Caleb Crowther, who had been the physician to the Wakefield Dispensary and House of Recovery, prior to it becoming Clayton Hospital. Although she described herself as an 'independent lady' in the 1851 census, she had an important role as the president of the House of Recovery, and oversaw a small committee of women who gave up their time to ensure the running of the hospital.

Mary Pilkington, sister of Sir Lionel Pilkington of Chevet Hall, whose occupation on the 1861 census is listed as 'Baronet's daughter', never married, but lived at Chevet with her brother and his wife and family until his death in 1901. When his heir, Sir Thomas Pilkington, took up residence with his wife, Lady Kathleen, Mary moved into Rock Cottage at Newmillerdam. Mary was very much involved in local life, and in 1863 paid for a village institute to be built. It was used as a reading room and night school. Prior to this she had established a National School at Walton in 1857, and added a Training, Laundry and Cookery School for girls in 1871.

Changes in women's working lives were slow in the late-nineteenth century, but the 1911 census tables, which recorded the occupations of males and females aged 10 years and upwards, reveal quite detailed information and show some advances were being made. Of the 20,610 women and girls within the district boundary, 14,610 were retired, unoccupied, wives or scholars. Of the 6,000 working women (twenty-nine per cent), 5,004 were unmarried, 373 widowed and 623 married (only just over ten per cent). Interestingly, there were 20,815 males recorded, 3,648 retired or with no occupation. Of the 17,167 men who were working it is not noted if they were married or otherwise.

Better-educated women were beginning to forge careers, with the proportion of women teachers and nurses now three times as high as 1861. Two women were recorded as physicians, plus a number of female business clerks in local and national government roles.

Regular work for girls and women

However, job opportunities hadn't changed much for the majority of women. Around thirty per cent were in some type of textile occupation, while garment-making and the provision of food and drink provided incomes for a further twenty per cent. The proportion of women in private domestic service in Wakefield had risen to nineteen per cent, with a further ten per cent in some cleaning, laundering or charring roles in hospitals and institutions. In these pre-Great War years grand homes such as Thornes House, owned by the Milnes-Gaskells, still had armies of servants running their households. The 1911 census shows Charles and Lady Catherine and their daughter Mary provided work for fifteen servants – from cook to scullery maid to footmen, although this was a reduction from 1891 when they had twenty staff, including a governess, butler and coachman. Chevet Hall, now home to Sir Thomas and Lady Kathleen Pilkington and their three children, was similar. Few of these girls and women were locally born and there must have been an interesting range of accents and upbringings, with girls from London, Shropshire, Devon and Kent working alongside Irish and Scots lasses.

Alternative opportunities to domestic service for less well-educated girls were presented in 1909, when Wm. Sugden and Sons, a company that had been producing garments since 1868, opened a new factory at Clarence Mills, Chald Lane, Wakefield, adding to its Barnsley shirt-production facilities. The company drew on the large numbers of single women – often miners' daughters – who lived locally. As well as garment-sewing the company provided a wide range of work in office roles for clerks and typists plus packing-room work. Apart from the management team and pattern-cutting (seen as a man's job for which night-school training was required), the workforce was predominantly female. Men who took jobs on the shop floor rarely lasted beyond six months, teased remorselessly by the women and ribbed by male colleagues for being 'cissies'.

Girls were recruited straight from school, with a personnel officer visiting various schools every term to choose twenty girls for training. The selection process was straightforward and comprised an eyesight test – 'what can you see in this photograph?' – and a dexterity test, where candidates were required to pick up pins (with each hand) and put them into a slot. According to their ability, girls were assigned to specific jobs and each underwent three months' training at Sugden's training school, learning to make one component part – sleeve, cuff, shirt body, buttonhole etc. – starting by sewing a line on paper, and turning a right angle corner, before progressing to sewing scraps of cloth and learning the intricacies of threading a machine.

There was a sense of Sugden's being a company that families stayed working for, a notion of belonging to the 'family'. Although it was an accepted rule for girls to give up work once married, the baton was passed down the generations, meaning Sugden's employed women whose grandmothers and mothers had each worked for the company in their turn. Women worked forty-eight hours over 5½ days, starting at 7.30 a.m., and were paid a base rate plus a bonus for achieving above a set target. It was 1949 before any girl earned £5 in a week. Those who did not achieve the target were disciplined. Wage negotiations were generally on a national level, leaving little room for discord, although occasional withdrawals of labour did occur, for instances such as heating breakdowns, where the women would down tools and gather in the canteen until 'it warms up'.

For those who wanted it, there was career progression. Women became supervisors, shop floor and quality control managers and pay increased accordingly. Overtime (paid at higher rates) was sometimes necessary, particularly during the First World War, when the company switched production to sew clothing for the armed forces.

Good supervision and close working relationships were key to productivity. A supervisor noticing a machinist's performance deteriorate could bring it to the attention of the female personnel officer, who encouraged the worker to discuss any problems. Often there were issues at home, or a girl might be pregnant. Having another woman as an unofficial counsellor often helped, and the company assisted with some problems, such as finding alternative accommodation for girls who were being abused at home.

This paternalistic approach extended beyond the factory floor. Sugden family events were celebrated with big dances in the works' canteen, to which employees and their families were invited. Workers reciprocated by having collections and presentations to the management – they enjoyed the act of giving.

Where anniversaries and birthdays coincided there was an even better excuse to celebrate. What a treat it must have been for the employees of all Sugden's factories to join the family in a day trip to Blackpool in July 1936. The reason cited was the coming of age of Mr Percy Sugden and the wedding anniversaries of his brother William and cousin Allen. Trains carrying the 1,300 employees from Wakefield, Barnsley and Cleckheaton left at 7.40 a.m., arriving in Blackpool at just after 11 a.m. Every item for the excursion had been considered and arranged for by the family, including a hearty three-course lunch at Blackpool Station restaurant – at which guests were invited to have a second helping of any or every course – and good weather! Return trains departed at 11.25 p.m., so one imagines 'a good time was had by all'.[7]

Christmas was another cause for merriment. The *Wakefield Express,* 21 December 1935, described the scene:

> The factory of Messrs Wm. Sugden and Sons Ltd, the well-known Wakefield manufacturers of shirting, shirts

and artisans' clothing, at present does not look like a workshop at all, but a scene out of a child's book, and the reason is that the employees, about 370 girls, have decorated the otherwise rather prosaic building with festoons, seasonable bunting, etc. The girls sit in rows of 38 all the way down the big workroom, and each row has kept to its own colour scheme. Red, blue, white, green, orange and pink are the predominating colours, and the upper reaches of the workroom are one mass of colour. The girls have captured the Christmas spirit to such an extent as to decorate their sewing machines and work with tinsel in their hair. There is not a lamp in the mill which is not covered with coloured paper, and from each lamp descends a cluster of balloons. The girls have subscribed to the cost among themselves, the directorate having nothing whatever to do with it, although it must be admitted that that austere group of gentlemen, with Mr W. B. Sugden representing Wakefield, have given them a free hand in the decorating and beautifying of the factory.

There were other social activities – bowling clubs and sports fields, netball and swimming clubs, regular outings and dances – all serving to enhance the lives of working women.

Prior to the Second World War, Sugden's introduced a holiday fund into which workers deposited a weekly amount for the company to invest on their behalf with a building society. A week before the annual fortnight's closure the money (many thousands of pounds) was withdrawn and distributed. At a time when many people lived hand-to-mouth and saved little, the holiday money must have been a wonderful bonus.

Isaak Donner and his wife Hermione (known as Herma) arrived in Wakefield in 1940. Born in Belz, Ukraine, but forced to move to Vienna in 1913, Isaak had been in business making shirts and, during the 1930s, was selling the products in an area stretching from western Austria, through Germany, Switzerland, Czechoslovakia and Romania. After Austria was annexed by Germany, the Jewish Donner family left for England. Through discussion with the Ministry of Labour, Isaak was given a choice of five towns in which to set up a clothing factory and selected Wakefield. Arriving at the railway station, he was greeted by a manager from the labour ministry, the local Midland Bank manager and two 'business angels', Mr Sharphouse, a grocer, and Mr Holdsworth, a woollen manufacturer, who invested in the business and helped find premises. One of the provisos in establishing the business was that it should provide employment for women. The *Yorkshire Post and Leeds Intelligencer* announced the 'work for 200 women at new Wakefield factory' in April 1940, revealing that the making of shirts for the home and export trade was to be added to Wakefield's industries at a new factory in Kirkgate, with machinery and plant due to arrive about 15 April. It added it would be necessary to train the women to be employed in the specialised work of making the shirt to be marketed, since it involved making a shirt with a collar renewal arrangement, which Mr Donner had patented. Selection of the workforce was through the Labour Exchange, where women's family circumstances – such as having children or being pregnant – were enquired into. By now, married women were being encouraged and welcomed into workforces.

The factory started small, in a top-floor room of the building on Kirkgate, with Herma working alongside her husband, sewing and cleaning. However, with cotton in short supply, instead of men's shirts the company made blouses out of parachute 'silk' viscose. As demand for workwear blouses grew with the increasing numbers of women entering the workplace to replace men serving in the war, the company gradually expanded, taking on more workers and occupying more space in the building.

From the start women were employed on an equal basis to men, with four hourly wage grades, according to age. Workers could start at 14 years old, but did not receive full pay until they reached their nineteenth birthday. Wages were similar to those paid to bus or truck drivers, but not as high as miners' wages (whose environment was far more dangerous). Ninety per cent of the workforce were miners' wives and daughters, brought into Wakefield from the local mining villages by a fleet of double-decker buses. It meant women could never be late for work – but of course could be absent if they missed the bus! Typically they worked forty-eight hours over 5½ days and there was plenty of overtime available, paying double rates on a Sunday. Groups of friends often volunteered for weekend work, giving themselves chance for good natter over lunch-break in the subsidised canteen. For many the work provided company, especially for those whose menfolk were away.

As well as operating sewing-machines (where the skills and faster work pace required earned the highest wages), women made up two-thirds of the warehouse workforce, though men were still expected to do heavy lifting. There was clerical work too, from invoicing to procurement to secretarial tasks, plus there were jobs in the pressing and cutting-rooms. A lady called Vi Dwyer ran the cutting-room and another lady, Eileen, was Isaak's PA and supervised the offices with a keen eye. Each line of machinists was overseen by a woman.

Only one job was considered solely a man's job – the band-knife cutting-machine. Not that women weren't capable of operating it, but it was dangerous and the company would not risk injury to women because of their importance in keeping their households going – an expectation that wasn't altered now they were working full-time as well.

Some women came to the fore as expert fundraisers, collecting money for the war effort, injured servicemen and other causes. The generosity was astounding, with many giving out of proportion to their means, though this may also have been a reflection of the fact that women now had their own income and could do with it as they pleased.

By 1945, the company occupied the whole Kirkgate building, working on a top-down manufacturing process – where everything travelled downwards towards the door, via lifts and chutes at each stage. By the end of the war there were

500 employees and with cotton fabric once more available, the company finally began production of its two-collar shirts – the Double Two.

The Double Two company provided good working conditions for its largely female workforce. There was a company doctor to look after employees' health – particularly to prevent women working too long into their pregnancies, there was a subsidised canteen to ensure they had a good meal each day, and a tea trolley for break times. A Christmas dinner with drinks for all staff was prepared and served by the all-male management team – who also washed up afterwards. Despite many women having supervisory roles, there were no women on the board of directors for another forty to fifty years. Many women did not seek promotion since they had enough responsibility running their homes, without added obligations at work.

However, men must have had to take some responsibility at home while some of Wakefield's women headed to London for the British Industries Fair, which ran from 3 to 14 May 1948:

> The Wakefield Double Two women had a chance to show off their skills to the world and continue the company's export drive when in 1948, thirty-four of them demonstrated their work for the benefit of overseas visitors to the British Industries Fair at Earl's Court. It was 'work as usual' on the specially assembled production line, where the team displayed its ability to produce a shirt with two collars every eighty seconds – equating to a weekly output of 1,600 shirts per team, still insufficient to keep abreast of global post-war demand. The girls stayed in a London hotel for the duration of the exhibition and the company gave them opportunity for sightseeing and fun. They were bitterly disappointed though when the anticipated visit to their stand by the king and queen did not materialise because the royal party was running forty minutes behind schedule.

Yorkshire Post and Leeds Intelligencer, 3 May 1948

Women's war work

As can be demonstrated from the 1911 census information, very few of Wakefield's married women worked prior to the First World War, but as the war progressed, the lives of women changed as they stepped into men's jobs to release more men to serve their country. Opportunities for women to take well-paid factory work were presented, as engineering companies switched from machine-making to munitions manufacture. One company that turned to making shells was E. Green's, established in Wakefield in 1845 to make 'The Green's Economiser', a device that economised energy usage by using waste heat from boilers to heat up the feed water. This was heavy engineering and few women worked at the company.

The particular war-work undertaken at Green's was the machining of shell blanks and copper bands, filling with bullets, fitting nosecaps and other requirements. Existing plant machinery was gradually adapted for war production, although some 'Economisers' were still built. The company let it be known that every eligible man must enlist for the forces – those exempted for medical reasons displayed a badge. With a much-reduced workforce the company received its first order for 5,000 two-inch Howitzer bombs in September 1915, followed by a further order for 1,000 three-inch Howitzers six weeks later. Just two women were recruited initially, taking jobs in the foundry. Four others attempted pit work, but were not strong enough. To test women's capabilities, 18-year-old Esme Tennant, daughter of Gilbert Tennant, the managing director, was asked to fill an eighteen-pound shrapnel shell – and having established that women could do this work, high-grade female labour was recruited. Green's operated three eight-hour shifts, with a woman supervisor for each shift. The company already had a canteen, built in 1905, and this facility became very popular with the workers, not only for the refreshments provided by Mrs Mary Ann Piper, the former caretaker turned canteen manager, but for the temporary relief from the strain of war. While men exchanged banter and read newspapers, the women knitted navy and khaki garments for the menfolk overseas and gossiped. A government inspector visiting Green's in 1916, observed that women, although unable to work pipe lathes, were suited to operating the electrical crane and many continued this work long after the war had ended.[8]

Working conditions for female munitions workers came under scrutiny in early 1916, when on Friday, 11 February, the Health of Munition Workers' committee issued two memoranda dealing with the employment of women and hours of work. Praising the universal response of women to the country's call for their help, the committee commented on the social and industrial significance of the extension of the employment of married women and young girls and the revival of the employment of women at night. Women and girls of every social grade had answered the country's call, including dressmakers, laundry-workers, textile-workers, domestic servants, clerical workers, assistants, and students, women and girls with no previous wage-earning experience and large numbers of soldiers' wives and widows. The committee's concerns related to the health and output of the workers and raised five matters demanding the careful attention of employers of women on a large scale. These were: the employment period; rest breaks and provision of meals; sanitary conditions in the factory; the women's physical condition and the management and supervision of this new workforce.

At the time there were three systems of employment of munitions workers being adopted: a 13–14 hour shift (including overtime), a twelve-hour shift, or an eight-hour shift. The shift patterns included the undesirable, but necessary, night shift. There were conflicting views on whether it was better to employ women on permanent night shifts, which brought its own issues, or whether to alternate day and night work – again a system that wasn't without disadvantage to the worker. It was also noted that some women were spending two to three hours each day travelling to and from work. The committee's recommendations included adopting an eight-hour shift (without overtime) where possible, as it yielded the best results longer-term, providing well-managed industrial canteens with good, wholesome food, and appointing forewomen, nurses, and welfare supervisors to ensure each woman worker had ready access to an officer of the same sex in case of difficulties with her work, health, or employment conditions. Where possible, women were to avoid lifting or carrying heavy objects and were not to subject themselves to sudden violent, physically unsuitable movements when operating machines.

One of the largest munitions factories in the area was Barnbow's at Crossgates in Leeds. Construction started in late 1915, and a large recruitment drive commenced. By October 1916, there were 16,000 employees, eventually nearly all women. Only a third came from Leeds, others travelled from Castleford, Pontefract, Wakefield and outlying villages, journeying to work on the thirty-eight daily trains specially chartered for the purpose.

As one newspaper correspondent later recalled, the 'Barnbow Specials', as they were known, contained an unrepressed and uninhibited collection of women. Returning from their nightshifts, 'they swept from the train like a pack of hounds, putting their arms round any men they could find and kissing them'. At least one luckless commercial traveller, who got on their train in error, was stripped naked and his clothes discarded by the time the train arrived at the factory, unable to alight until someone brought him a blanket to cover his modesty. Porters were deployed to 'do the Barnbow windows' – close those left open and report any damage – 'it was like sweeping up after a hundred jumble sales'.

These high jinks were probably a release after a hard night's physical work, but there were concerns about the levels of drunkenness throughout the country during the First World War. In late 1915, a Central Control Board for liquor traffic was set up to apply drastic regulations to scheduled districts, curbing the hours during which liquor could be sold. Special restrictions on spirits were introduced, with treating and credit prohibited. Violators faced severe punishment of £100 fines and six months' hard labour. Anticipating the schedule might be applied to the West Riding, local enquiries were carried out, which revealed that in most towns and occupations, instances of drunkenness had reduced as the people worked earnestly for the war effort – by twenty-three per cent in Bradford. Wakefield, however, had a different story to tell. Existing restrictions had little restraining effect, with the same amount of consumption being packed into a shorter space of time, and women indulging much more freely than before. This may have been related in part to the increase in disposable income the women of Wakefield were now experiencing. The chief constable urged for public houses to close an hour earlier and open later in the morning to prevent early tippling.

It seems the recommendations of the Health of Munition Workers' committee were heeded as regards hours of work and travelling distances, since the following advertisement appeared in the *Yorkshire Post and Leeds Intelligencer* on 16 August 1916:

> MUNITIONS— Position open to educated, patriotic British Women, of good class, anxious to serve their country in the present, great struggle. The work is responsible, but not arduous; hours short; remuneration good; persons resident more than 10 miles away, or already engaged on Government work, will not be engaged.

What the advertisement failed to mention was the physical danger in handling explosive materials. Naturally cigarettes were banned, as were hairpins and combs. Women wore only underwear beneath the uniform of a buttonless smock and cap, and for safety wore rubber-soled shoes. The Barnbow factory had its own herd of cows to provide milk for the women, who were encouraged to drink unlimited quantities as a protection against the skin-yellowing effects of handling cordite.

At around 10.30 p.m. on 5 December 1916, shortly after the night shift commenced, a huge explosion in the shell-filling room at Barnbow's killed thirty-five women instantly and maimed several others. One of the girls killed that night was Jennie Blackamore, the 21-year-old daughter of George and Sarah Ann Blackamore of Normanton. In 1911 Jennie (also known as Jane) was working as a general domestic servant at the Leeds City Hospital at Seacroft. It is not possible to determine whether she moved from her hospital job to work as a shell-filler only half-a-mile down the road, but although the munitions works was better paid it cost Jennie her life. Jennie was buried at All Saints, Normanton, on 11 December.

Women employed in munitions were initially paid lower wages than men, but negotiations at one munitions factory in April 1916, resulted in women's wages being raised to twenty shillings a week; still lower than the men's rate but with the same bonuses as men for piecework and overtime.

A national order was given by the Ministry of Munitions in February 1917, announcing women munitions workers in skilled jobs were to be paid twenty-five shillings a week for the first five weeks, then increasing by increments to 10½d per hour by the thirteenth week. For a forty-eight hour week this meant a forty-two shillings flat rate, plus of course any bonuses.

Keen to part the women from their good wages were the skin-cream manufacturers, who had previously pitched their products at 'society ladies' with money to spend on more luxurious skin preparations than soap and water. Seizing the opportunity, their newspaper adverts targeted a new market:

WOMEN MUNITION WORKERS. A WARNING

One has only to stand at the gates of any large munition factory employing women, and watch them coming out, to realise that a few months at such work, under such conditions, will mean the ruin of most complexions. Those which escape will be the ones that have been properly protected against the vitiating effect of long and laborious hours in a dust-laden atmosphere. Fortunately it is a simple enough matter both to prevent the mischief and to repair it. As many women have found out already, the nightly use of Pomeroy Skin Food, by keeping the skin clean, soft, and supple, prevents that loss of facial charm which usually results from working in a factory. It nourishes the skin, but does not in any way encourage the growth of superfluous hair. An eighteen penny jar of Pomeroy Skin Food from the chemist will last one quite a long time, and abundantly prove its great value to those who desire to look their best.

Sheffield Daily Telegraph, 13 April 1916

There was competition:

WOMEN WAR-WORKERS! VEN-YUSA Brings Back the Bloom to Your Cheeks.

Munition-workers find Ven-Yusa a boon for restoring their complexions. There is no reason why a woman's complexion should be ruined by war-work in either munition factory or the land. The regular use of Ven-Yusa, the oxygen face cream, is all that is required to preserve the natural, delicate beauty of the skin. Being so invigorating and revitalising, Ven-Yusa is precisely the preparation so much needed at this trying time. It gives the skin what is aptly described as "oxygen bath,' putting into it more life and more lustre. It restores that velvety softness of youth, and guards the complexion from the harmful effects of mental and bodily fatigue. Ven-Yusa is perfectly greaseless, and has a charm and utility all of its own. Try it on your own skin. You will gratified with the result. – 1 shilling per jar from Chemists, or direct from C. E. Fulford, Ltd., Leeds.

Hull Daily Mail, 1 August 1916

∞

Just as there was a drive to get women working in the factories, there was need for women to work on farms.

The meeting of the West Riding Agricultural committee in Wakefield on 1 March 1916, was attended by two representatives of the West Riding Women's Committee, Lady Catherine Milnes-Gaskell and Lady Evelyn Collins (daughter of the Duke of Roxburghe). A letter from Lord Selborne regarding 'further co-operation in improving the efficiency of the arrangements for encouraging the employment of women the land' was discussed. Lady Collins said that as far as her experience went, the idea of employing women on the farm had not been well-received by farmers, nor had the women come forward as readily as they ought to have done. Lady Milnes-Gaskell remarked that although farmers were hostile, she did not despair of the scheme for the employment of women, and she was doing all she could to promote it. However, no resolution was passed. (*Yorkshire Post and Leeds Intelligencer*, 2 March 1916)

A further meeting, this time with farmers themselves, took place in August 1916, when Miss Georgina Binnie Clark, Agricultural Labour Organiser for the West Riding, spoke about the employment of women on farms. Miss Clark, a Dorset woman by birth, had set up her own farm in Canada (against much opposition) but had been very successful. An ardent feminist, she was keen to promote the splendid opportunities that careers in agriculture could provide for women and said it was time the women of England came forward to demonstrate what they could do on the land. Miss Clark claimed that although the wages in munitions works might be more attractive, there was nothing at the end of it – unlike farming. The meeting's chairman agreed, noting there was no doubt that whatever women did in times of peace, in time of war they were able to do almost anything a man could do, and it had been proved they were able to help in almost all farming operations. All that was wanted was a little goodwill, a little patriotism, a little practice, and suitable dress.

However, the long-term opportunities for women in farming were disputed at a horticultural experts' conference in October 1916. A paper, *Lady Gardeners*, presented gardening as a happy and health-giving occupation for women and urged educated women to train as head gardeners, where there were openings with salaries ranging from £100 to £150 per year.

> It was a mistake to encourage women to suppose that there was permanent work awaiting them on the

land. But in the higher branches of horticulture it was different. Here there would be in future less of swear and sweat, and more of brains; and therein women would no doubt find a sphere.

Yorkshire Post and Leeds Intelligencer, 12 October 1916

In April 1917, an appeal was made for at least 1,500 sturdy women of the West Riding to come forward for agricultural work to replace men due to be called up. This specific appeal was expected to bring better results than previous more general appeals, where tens of thousands of women had registered to work towards the war effort, only to find there was nothing for them to do. Since such vague appeals provoked a spirit of restlessness, this time the work would be already lined up for them. To offer reassurance to girls leaving home to work on the land the Women's War Agricultural Committee of the West Riding had systems in place to look after them, and every applicant was examined by a doctor to ensure she was fit enough to start. Pay was at least eighteen shillings a week and workwear provided. The results were not immediate, partly because women thought the work degrading, and partly due to prejudice by some farmers. Of course, not all farmers were reluctant to employ women. Mr Thompson of East Rigton near Harrogate, having had up to thirty women working on his farm at any one time, was a most ardent advocate for their employment, and Mr Holgate of Scarcroft near Leeds also spoke highly of their labour, but added that women needed to be convinced their services were required and suitable work could be found for them.

With discussions still ongoing about women as agricultural workers, a meeting at Wakefield's Corn Exchange in May 1917, considered the question of increased corn production and the government's requirement of a further 100,000 acres of the West Riding to be turned over to arable land. Lady Milnes-Gaskell urgently appealed once again to the West Riding farmers to utilise female labour and said she failed to understand why English women, like women in other countries, should not prove of real value on the land (*Yorkshire Post and Leeds Intelligencer,* 26 May 1917).

Farmers must have been eventually persuaded to employ women as agricultural workers, as around 16,000 were engaged during the First World War. However, few individual records remain. At the outbreak of the Second World War in 1939, women were once again called upon to help with the war effort by joining the Women's Land Army. Of course, many farmers still did not think it possible to employ girls, but soon overcame their prejudices when they saw how smartly the girls could work.

One letter from a Ripon farmer to the *Yorkshire Post and Leeds Intelligencer* in February 1940, was full of praise for his new employee:

> In January I engaged a young woman, 19 years old, strongly built (an artist by profession) and I have yet to find a youth of similar age, although trained in farm work since leaving school, who could equal her, with the exception of ploughing, in which she has yet to be tried. In one of the worst winters in living memory this girl has had entire charge of 120 pigs, with assistance in feeding only. She has folded sheep and hand-chopped turnip for them. She does all the cleaning out. She can take a horse and cart and load with manure and spread it on the land. I should not have expected more from a youth of 19. The girl has brains and uses them. I have not to be always prompting her. I feel sure there are many capable and willing girls in the Women's Land Army only too eager to do their duty if we only have the patience to train and try them.

Women were paid directly by the farmers for whom they worked – a minimum of 28 shillings for a forty-eight to fifty-hour week – with Sundays free. A deduction of 14 shillings was made from their pay to cover board and lodgings. Male agricultural workers were paid 38 shillings for the same job. There was no holiday, either unpaid or paid, until 1943, when the Land Girls' Charter introduced one week's holiday per year and raised the minimum wage to a net 22s 6d (after deductions for board etc.) for women over 18, and 18 shillings for 17 to 18 year olds.

One of the issues preventing farmers from employing girls was lack of accommodation. In response, hostels were built to house groups of women, usually about forty or so, who had left their homes to work in other counties. Yorkshire had around 5,500 land girls employed in its fields, and Yorkshire girls were gaining a fine reputation as the best workers in other counties too. In summer 1943, it was reported that every county in England and Wales had at least one contingent of Yorkshire girls, with 100–200 girls being 'exported' every week as war agricultural committees in every county asked for more.

A report from the *Yorkshire Post and Leeds Intelligencer*, 4 May 1943, describes how Yorkshire lasses were making their mark near Grantham in Lincolnshire:

> Little Ponton Angels (as the village calls them) are 36 fine, hard-working, wind-tanned land girls, mostly from Yorkshire, who help to solve the problems of the Lincolnshire farmers as their war service. They live in a Women's Land Army Hostel at Little Ponton, near Grantham, and go out each day, Sundays excepted, to variety of jobs on the land from fruit farming to tractor driving. A little more than a year ago the hostel was only being built and the girls were still at home and in their peace time jobs in West Riding towns. Nellie Smith, of 21, Stanmore Drive, Leeds, now driving a tractor, was a weaver: Margaret Casson of 72, Sands Rd. Dewsbury, who is now a shepherd was a blouse machinist: and Susan Cusworth, Park View, Hemingfield, now looking after a market garden, was a mantle alteration hand. The girls have become used to hard manual work, experienced many different branches of farm work, and hardened to all sorts of weather, working five and half days week, 51 weeks of the year. Up at 6.30am many of

the girls have two or three miles to cycle to work, and only the wettest weather keeps them off the land. Their hours vary with the season and the urgency of the work. During harvest they regularly work until dusk.

The general farm hands like [...] Audrey Wilkinson, Montague Street, Wakefield [...] undertake many jobs, from tending livestock to potato picking, and threshing—one of the hardest jobs of all, the girls say. Olga Lickley, formerly a typist in Leeds, was called upon this year to help with the lambing and liked it. Kathleen Murphy, of Neal Street, Bradford looks after fruit trees, pruning and spraying them, and collecting the harvest. The tractor drivers [...] move from farm to farm with their machines helping the farmers with ploughing, sowing, reaping or threshing as the season demands. Sometimes the girls get an SOS to go along in a body to help with potato picking, a back-breaking job.

In the hostel, a one-storey building on strictly utilitarian lines, the girls live together in a jolly community family atmosphere, sharing certain duties, working together for entertainments and war charities and taking part in village life. They are mothered by the warden, Mrs G. Turner, who spares no effort to see that the girls are happy, comfortable, well fed and healthy. The leader, Margaret Foreman, is a London girl who has had considerable experience of the WLA since she left her post as a London shop assistant. The hostel itself is a cosy little place with its cream and green paint, and its decorations of massed spring flowers, many of them a regular gift from the Hall. Two signed photographs of the King and Queen are prominently displayed in the common room and are a matter of special pride to the girls ...

The girls believe in making most of their pleasures and interests a contribution to the war effort and in their spare time they organise whist drives and dances to raise money for the Prisoners of War Fund and the Merchant

Navy, inviting the villagers to join them. They contribute to the Red Cross Penny-a-Week Fund and have their own Savings Group. From time to time an Ensa party, or film show visits the hostel to give the girls a change. Last Sunday the girls turned out for a church parade, and they swung smartly through the leafy twisting lanes to the little Norman church on the hill. A dozen or so have formed a choir and sing in the church every Sunday. At Christmas all the girls and the Warden turned out for carol singing. A kitchen garden behind the hostel helps to supply fresh vegetables and salads, and hens keep the hostel supplied with eggs. Vicky Bird, of Ravensthorpe has her particular hobby, looking after Ginger and Freddie, two cuddly young rabbits she bought from a farm boy, and Edgar, a black cat who earns his keep mouse-catching. The girls enjoy their work and put their backs into it, but they are a little disappointed that they are not always appreciated. They think that the other women's services are given more of the limelight and the praise. They would like a little more leave (they get only seven days a year), particularly as it would be possible during certain slack periods – and they would like to have more than one railway warrant, that they might get home on Sundays from time to time. But these little grievances do not stop them from working hard and conscientiously at a job which they know is of paramount importance.

Four women 'exported' from Wakefield were Mary Fox, Doris Hampshire, Violet Lee and Doreen Pitchforth. Mary was only 18 when she was sent to Elstow near Bedford. Surprised to be away from home at such a young age she had to undertake the heavy work of harvesting crops, digging and muck-spreading, which she thoroughly enjoyed. Young and green when she started, by the end of the war she was 'well and truly educated' by the girls she had mixed with. Doris signed up in 1943, aged 20, and was sent to Glasbury-on-Wye in Herefordshire. Her work varied hugely – one day picking daffodils, the next spreading manure and lime. One of her favourite jobs was tractor-driving and she was reluctant to return to Wakefield at the end of the war. Violet joined the Land Army in 1941, and was sent first to an orchard at Surfleet in Lincolnshire, before being transferred to Wetherby Grange to fulfil her wish to be involved in dairy farming. Having never been near a cow before, it was a shock on her first morning to have to deal with a cow in labour, but she soon found her feet and began to enjoy rural life. Doreen had never left Wakefield and was only 14 when she was sent to Bury St Edmunds in 1943. She found the work extremely hard, but as she learned to drive a tractor and tend horses she began to love the way of life and stayed on for a year after the war ended.[9]

One Wakefield woman's thirst for adventure was finally quenched when she joined the WLA. Gladys Vollands, of Woodbine Terrace, was involved in various work at the beginning of the war. Immediately war broke out she and her sisters were called upon to help with meals for soldiers billeted at Unity Hall. She later volunteered for the national fire service, but again found herself doing the catering. Finally in 1943, she answered the call for more women to come forward for the WLA and joined thirty other young women to live at the WLA hostel on Oswin Avenue in Doncaster. From there, women were sent to any farm within a 20-mile radius to work for a day or two at a time, or longer. Sometimes girls were despatched to country house estates to help with forestry, or to market gardens to help with sterilising soil in greenhouses by digging trenches through which steam could be pumped. Some girls found themselves working alongside the German and Italian prisoners of war who were housed at a camp at Doncaster racecourse, and who, like the WLA, were drafted to work wherever they were needed on the land.[10]

Of course women were seconded into men's jobs closer to home. Even women with children, whose careers had been surrendered at marriage, were now needed in the workplace. But who would look after the children?

Recognising the need to mobilise married women, the Ministry of Labour instigated the provision of wartime nurseries to care for children up to 5 years old. The Treasury guaranteed the full cost of their building and equipping, plus the full cost of running the nurseries. Originally established for mothers who were working in munitions factories, the scheme was extended in June 1941, to include women who worked all day in any employment. A daily contribution of 3d per child (without meals) or 1s (with meals) was paid by the mothers.

Wakefield Council established two wartime nurseries. The first, at Burneytops, 5, West Parade, accommodated children overnight as well as during the day and opened 24 July 1942 and the second opened at Hall Rd, Lupset, two months later on 28 September. The two nurseries each looked after around thirty children during the day, with around a dozen spending nights at Burneytops. All staff were employed on temporary contracts not exceeding two years, and there appears to have been a high turnover, particularly at Burneytops. The first two matrons were Miss Lilian Green of Sharlston for Burneytops, and Mrs Ena Crayford for Lupset. Other matrons and deputy matrons (resident and non-resident) who came and went at Burneytops included Mrs G.H. Field, Mrs M.A. Taylor, Mrs H. Griffiths, Miss Ellen Martin, Miss Florence Mailing and Eileen Mosley. There were several other grades of staff – nursery nurses, probationer nurses, cooks, cleaners and laundresses, (see Appendix 2) but staffing became such a problem after Mrs Field went absent from 6 September and walked out four days later, that Burneytops had to close at night between 15 and 24 September 1943. Whether the issues were related to other staff is not clear, but the medical officer, recognising some (unrecorded) difficulties, authorised matrons at both sites to make their own appointments.[11]

When the war ended, both the matron and deputy matron at Lupset resigned. Nobody wanted to take their places, so with staffing difficulties once again a problem for the council, and communication from the ministry of health suggesting there was no longer justification to keep the nursery open, it closed. Remaining staff were transferred to Burneytops, which continued its role in providing much-needed childcare for working mothers until at least 1966.

CHAPTER FOUR

Wakefield's Women in the Professions

For well-educated women wanting a career with genuine prospects and challenges, there were two clear paths – nursing and teaching.

Nursing as a career

When Wakefield's two hospitals (the Dispensary and the House of Recovery) merged to become Clayton Hospital in 1854, Matron Mary Hudson stayed in charge until July 1856. Seeking her replacement, an advertisement was placed in the *Leeds Intelligencer* for 'an experienced and respectable woman without a family, but preferably married', to become the new matron. The duties included nursing and general management of the house, for which she would be paid £40 per year plus residence, coals, gas and water. Candidates were expected to attend for an interview at the hospital at twelve o' clock on 7 July, at which time the appointment would be made. The advert stipulated no travelling expenses would be allowed. There were ten candidates on the day, and from a shortlist of two – Mrs Sarah Oxley of Providence Street and Mrs Gill, a shopkeeper of Northgate – the former was appointed. Interestingly, Mrs Oxley's husband, Joseph joined her as a hospital servant, suggesting her career was the more important.

As the population increased, so did its healthcare needs. A new Clayton Hospital was built to include accident and special wards, an operating theatre, day rooms, an outpatients department and accommodation for sixty-two patients. It was officially opened on Wednesday, 30 July 1879. Its matron in 1881 was Miss Ellen Andrews of Aylesbury, Buckinghamshire and in 1891, Miss Jessie Johnston Hunter from Sunderland, who later became matron at Oldham Royal Infirmary.

By 1892, Miss Amy Eaton, who had qualified and worked in her home town of Derby between 1881 and 1889, was in charge. Clearly an ambitious woman, prepared to relocate to progress her career, she spent a year as a sister at the Royal Albert Hospital at Devonport before moving on in June 1890, to become night superintendent in Bristol. There she was promoted to assistant matron, and remained in post until November 1892, thence to Wakefield to run Clayton Hospital.[12] By 1901, she was in charge of fourteen nursing staff. Some, like Jane Phelps from Birmingham, were already qualified, experienced nurses. Others like Phoebe Coldwell (Holmfirth) Dorothy Henderson (Whitby) and Emily Bolland (Bradford) were probationers who were trained and attended lectures at the hospital for three years.

Miss Eaton left the hospital in 1902, to take up a post as superintendent of the Wakefield Medical, Surgical and Nurses' Home at 2, Wentworth Terrace, Wakefield. This institution supplied 'medical, surgical, mental, monthly, massage nurses at shortest notice' from its bank of sixteen nurses, charging £1 5s for ordinary cases and £1 11s 6d for infectious patients. It also received patients in the home at costs starting at £3 3s for a bed. Its nurses were paid £32 to £35 a year.

By 1905, Clayton hospital had eighty-five beds, staffed by a matron (Theodora Mary Pressland), four sisters, a staff nurse and nine probationers.[13] Theodora was a farmer's daughter, born in Bedfordshire and raised in Northamptonshire. Like Amy Eaton, she was well experienced and had worked her way up through her career at various hospitals, including being assistant matron at Newcastle Royal Infirmary and matron at Durham County Hospital. The census of 1911 shows very few of the twenty-five nursing staff and ward maids were local women, but most of the fourteen supporting staff of laundry maids and kitchen staff were. All were single and all lived-in.

Two of the ward maids, Fanny Tennant from Staffordshire and Nellie Clayton from Pateley Bridge, went on to train at the Wakefield Union Infirmary and the West Riding Asylum respectively. Theodora died in 1921, still in her post, and was succeeded by Miss A. Cameron and an assistant matron, Miss A. Linton. By this time the hospital had further expanded and had 108 beds. Nursing staff had increased accordingly and the eight sisters and thirty nurses usually had around eighty-nine patients to care for.[14]

Women who chose nursing as a career underwent a three-year training period as probationer nurses. Candidates were required to be aged 20–27 and well educated. They lived-in, and in 1899 were paid £16, £18 and £20 accordingly for each of their three years' training. Those who passed the training were awarded a certificate of nursing. By 1920, probationer nurses at Clayton were being paid £20, £25 and £30 (*Yorkshire Post and Leeds Intelligencer,* 10 November 1920) and pay rates continued to rise. In 1936, the County Hospital, Wakefield, also a recognised training school for nurses, offered salaries of £30 for first year, £38 for second year and £45 for third year, with the usual residential allowances. By 1943, the criteria had changed and Clayton Hospital was advertising for women aged 18–30 to train for four years at a starting salary of £30, rising to £50.

Student nurses' wages and conditions changed considerably once the NHS was established in 1948. An advertisement in February 1949, for female student nurses to train for caring for patients with nervous and mental disorders at Stanley Royd Hospital, offered a cash training allowance of £235 per year, with a proficiency allowance of £20 on passing the preliminary state exam and an allowance of £240 in year two. In the third year they received £255 plus a proficiency award of £30 for completing the year or on passing the final state exam. Those who passed the final exam were automatically promoted to Staff Nurse. Students could live in or out, with resident students charged £100 per year for board and lodgings. To encourage married women to train there was an allowance paid to those with family responsibilities. All meals on duty were provided.

Accommodation for nurses also improved over time. In 1902, a new wing was added to Clayton Hospital purely for the nursing staff. Named the Shaw Nurses' Home after its benefactor (Mr Joseph Shaw, a wine and spirit merchant of Sandal, who left £80,000 to the hospital), it had twenty bedrooms and a dining room and sitting room (*Leeds Mercury,* 26 May 1902). A further nurses' home was built at St John's in the 1920s as a memorial to those who had lost their lives in the First World War. Its foundation stone was laid on 14 November 1923, by Princess Mary and two years later the Nurses' Memorial Hostel was opened as part of the Armistice Day commemorations on Wednesday, 11 November 1925, by Lady Pilkington of Chevet Hall.

A report in the *Yorkshire Evening Post* in May 1949, revealed further improvements to conditions. Wakefield's nurses were to get a room each. Dormitories at Pinderfields Hospital were being converted to individual bed-sitting rooms, with 'divan beds, bedside lamps, plastic-topped dressing tables and plenty of wardrobe space'. Alderman Mrs M.L. Thomas, vice-chair of the Wakefield 'B' Group Hospital Management Committee and WVS organiser, was in charge of colour schemes, and hoped to have East and West cottages finished by July. A third, twenty-nine room, nurses' home at Stanley Hall was also being planned. Miss E.G. Burton, matron at the County Hospital was transferred as matron for the larger hospital at Pinderfields and a recruitment drive (perhaps boosted by the new accommodation) to appoint a further 100 nurses was underway. Even in the early days of the NHS nursing shortages meant only 400 of the 700 beds at Pinderfields were in use.

∞

That nursing was a highly regarded occupation was left in no doubt, when Colonel Bernard Haigh of Milnthorpe Grange at Sandal made one nurse a beneficiary in his will. The colonel, who had sustained a long illness, left £6,000 to Nurse F.B. Marley 'in slight recognition of her care and devotion' when he passed away in September 1939. To put this into context, he left

£100 to Eva Steele, his cook, and £50 to his chauffeur (*Yorkshire Evening Post,* 12 December 1939).

Prior to this generous bequest, the value of women as nurses had been emphasised during the First World War. When, in 1914, the call came for extra women to train or volunteer for nursing duties at home and abroad to deal with the growing workload of utterly distressing cases, Wakefield's women stepped up.

Nurses recruited to the Queen Alexandra's Imperial Military Nursing Service (QAIMNS) were despatched to the theatres of war, including France, Gallipoli, Mesopotamia and Salonika. In addition were the QAIMNS Reserve and the Territorial Force Nursing Service (TFNS), mainly working in territorial hospitals controlled by the War Office. Not only were women needed in the military hospitals at home and abroad but in provincial hospitals too. Unemployed trained nurses at home were encouraged to return to care for the growing number of men being sent back to Britain for treatment.

Also helping sick and wounded soldiers were women who joined the Voluntary Aid Detachment (VAD). Originally formed in 1909, for the purpose of providing nursing and medical assistance in times of war, VAD women also worked as cooks, ambulance drivers, quartermasters and letter-writers, mainly in the wards of auxiliary, convalescent and military hospitals, although some went abroad to work in casualty clearing stations, field hospitals and base hospitals. The British Red Cross oversaw the deployment of trained nurses abroad during the First World War and many of those 2,000 nurses who offered their services at the outbreak refused a salary. By mid-1915 they were being joined by partially trained VADs who undertook less technical duties.

Three trained nurses from Wakefield stand out. Florence Dixon trained as a nurse at Clayton Hospital under Theodora Pressland, receiving her certification in 1912, aged 19. In 1913, she transferred to Hull Royal Infirmary as a staff nurse and was promoted to sister in 1914. On 20 December 1916, now a sister at Ashton-under-Lyme District Infirmary, she applied to join the QAIMNS Reserve. On 7 February 1917, Florence was posted as a staff nurse at the King George V Military Hospital in Dublin, until sent to India on 15 April 1918. Her original contract was for two years, and she signed up for a further two-year period on 23 December 1919, transferring to Basra, Mesopotamia, until demobilisation in February 1920. Arriving back in Britain in April, she had a month's leave before taking a new position at the Royal Arsenal Hospital at Woolwich at a salary of £68 per year, plus a £20 service bonus, living in the sisters' quarters. The reference written by the principal matron of No 3 British General Hospital said Florence had proved herself a good nurse, most likeable, tactful, kind and considerate to her patients. She finally left the QAIMNS Reserve in August 1921, taking a position as sister in charge of a men's ward at the West End Hospital, Gloucester Gate, London. After leaving nursing to marry in September 1924, and her Air Ministry husband being posted abroad without her, Florence applied to be taken back onto the reserve for a short period as she had nothing to do. But since she was now a married woman, her request was declined. In 1939, she and her husband were living in Cirencester, Gloucestershire, with her occupation given as 'unpaid domestic duties, state registered nurse'. It appears there were no children.

Minnie Wood, whose parents lived on Agbrigg Road, Sandal, trained as a nurse in Salford, becoming sister in a men's surgical ward in July 1911, before applying to join the QAIMNS in November, aged 30. Minnie was initially deployed in London, but in 1916 her war service intensified, when she was sent first to No 14 Stationary Hospital in Boulogne, which treated men with infectious diseases, and then to 25 General Hospital at Hardelot. From there she went to work with a field ambulance, then moved between various hospitals and casualty clearing stations for a further year. She was promoted to sister on 18 May 1917, and by August was in charge of Casualty Clearing Station 44 at Brandhoek, between Ypres and Poperinge. Specialising in treating chest and abdominal wounds, No 44 CCS was relatively close to the front lines and within range of the larger German guns. At 10 a.m. on 21 August, shells started to fall on the CCS. According to another sister, Kate (Kathryn Evelyn) Luard, who gave an account of the disaster in a letter home, one shell crashed close to the sisters' quarters, wrecking the tents and blasting shrapnel everywhere. Five nurses were wounded, one very seriously by shrapnel, which passed through her from back to front. Minnie Wood cradled her for twenty minutes until she passed away. That nurse was Staff Nurse Nellie Spindler, of 104, Stanley Road, Wakefield.

Born 10 August 1889, Nellie attended Eastmoor Council School before working at Wakefield corporation infectious diseases hospital in Park Lane, under Matron Beatrice Whitham from 1910–12. Her formal nursing training was at Leeds Beckett Military Hospital, where she qualified in 1915. In October that year she enlisted for the QAIMNS Reserve. She spent her first eighteen months' service at a military hospital in Lichfield, before being posted to No 42 Stationary Hospital in May 1917. On 7 August she joined the 44 CCS with Minnie at its new location in Brandhoek.

After the shelling, the station was evacuated and moved, with 320 patients, to Lijssenthoek, 8 km west. Nellie was buried there, with full military honours, on 22 August 1917, the only female casualty of the Battle of Passchendaele.

On 22 October 1917, the *Leeds Mercury* reported the 'brave Wakefield nurse' Minnie Wood had been awarded the Military Medal. The *London Gazette*, 17 October citation stated:

> For most courageous devotion to duty. On the 21st August 1917, this lady was Sister-in-Charge at No. 44 Casualty Clearing Station, Brandhoek, when it was shelled at short intervals from 11 a.m. till night, one Sister being killed. This lady never lost her nerve for a moment and during the whole of a most trying day, carried out her duties with the greatest steadiness and coolness. By her work and example she greatly assisted in the speedy evacuation of the patients and the transfer of the sisters.

Minnie's nursing continued throughout the war, mainly at casualty clearing stations. She was awarded the Royal Red Cross first and second class, mentioned in despatches three times and in June 1919, was awarded the OBE for her services. By July, exhausted, debilitated and anaemic, she was sent to Craiglands Hydro in Ilkley to recuperate. Once recovered she served a further 4½ years with the QAIMNS, in Devonport, Lichfield, Malta and Belfast, before resigning on 31 January 1924 for family and personal reasons. In recognition of her distinguished service during the First World War, she was allowed to retain her Queen Alexandra's Nurse badge.

The women of Wakefield also played their part as VADs, not only in the two auxiliary military hospitals in the city (St John's/Clayton and Park Lane/White Rose) but also further afield. St John's was created at Wentworth House, when the War Office, needing additional provision for treating soldiers at Clayton, took over the Girls' High School's building. There were three wards, Wellington, Kitchener and Roberts, with an operating theatre in the room opposite and its full title was St John's Auxiliary Military Hospital at Wentworth House, Wakefield (St John's).

Some of Wakefield's VADs enlisted as volunteers between 1910 and 1913 and many were old girls of the high school. Mrs Ellen (Nellie) King, of Belgrave Mount, Pinderfields, who enrolled on 17 December 1910, was the Wakefield VAD commandant. Her profession as a head teacher probably helped! Annie Gloyne and her married sister Mabel Cameron, also two of the first members, were schoolmistresses, but both became part-time voluntary nursing sisters at St John's for the duration of the war. Another, younger, sister, Constance Gloyne joined the VAD in September 1915 and completed 780 hours voluntary work at St John's, followed by a year at a military hospital in France and a further two years at Tidworth Military Hospital, Salisbury.

In March 1915, with demand for trained nurses rapidly growing, the army medical authorities agreed to take VAD nurses into the military hospitals for a month's training, providing they were recommended by their matron. Prior to being accepted as probationers the women had to obtain both

First Aid and Home Nursing certificates. To enable more VADs to qualify for training, the St John's Association rapidly arranged a number of emergency examinations for potential candidates.

Like Constance Gloyne, Clarice Abbishaw, working as a furniture shop assistant in 1911, took the opportunity to train and was engaged as a paid nurse at Leeds Beckett Military Hospital, before going to a general hospital in Rouen, France (with the TFNS) for nine months, just as the war ended. Another girl, Maggie Charlesworth, who in 1911 was working as a warehouse girl, trained at Ripon for two years and spent eight months at a French military hospital.

Women who otherwise may never have worked also found useful occupation in the VAD. Seventeen-year old Phyllis Pilkington, daughter of Sir Thomas and Lady Kathleen of Chevet Hall, and 39-year-old Frances Elizabeth Percy Tew, daughter of banker Percy Tew of Heath Hall, both volunteered in August 1914, and each carried out more than 8,000 hours of nursing duties at St John's and Darrington Convalescent Hospitals until February 1919, practically full-time work. In recognition of her work, Frances was awarded the Royal Red Cross (second-class) in August 1919.[15]

Similarly Lady Catherine Milnes-Gaskell and her daughter Lady Constance worked tirelessly for the cause. Lady Catherine became vice-president of both Clayton VAD and Field House Auxiliary Hospital in Bradford, and Constance commandant of the Tyrone VAD. In January 1916 they were both promoted to Ladies of Justice in the Order of the Hospital of St John of Jerusalem, an honour bestowed by the king. (See Appendix 3 for list of VAD.)

Women as teachers

That Wakefield's women were valued as educators was demonstrated by the choice of the Wakefield School Board's emblem in 1872, which depicted a central female figure surrounded by three children whom she was instructing.

Teaching offered women opportunity to progress, both financially through regular salary increases and in status through merit-based promotion, which created some semblance of equality for men and women teachers (although equal pay was some way off). However, for a long period, one key inequality was the discontinuation of a woman's employment once she married.

The question of married female teachers was raised at a Wakefield education committee meeting in September 1907, when it was agreed all future appointments of female teachers would be on the proviso that their contract would be terminated *ipso facto* on their marriage, and all female teachers employed by Wakefield's authority would have to give a minimum month's notice of their intention to marry. The rule did not apply to existing married female teachers and the committee reserved a power of discretion in appointing married women. Nonetheless it was a generally held rule and perhaps one that deterred many women from marrying. It was a stark choice – career or marriage and a family.

In the 1870s, girls wishing to become teachers started at the age of 13 or 14 as monitors before serving a four-year term as a pupil teacher, in which they received on-the-job training and special tuition from the head teacher in the morning pre-school and at lunchtime, at a starting salary of £10 a year. They took examinations in subjects including arithmetic, geography, history, reading and needlework and spent another year as an 'ex-pupil teacher' taking further qualifications to become a certificated assistant teacher. Having trained and worked hard to achieve a career, status and good salary, it was a lot to give up.

Louisa Haliday, born in Wakefield in 1854, trained as a pupil teacher in an elementary school in Manchester, before returning to the West Riding in 1874, to be an assistant teacher with her older sister Elizabeth, recently appointed headmistress of Moldgreen elementary school in Huddersfield at £100 per year. Elizabeth wasn't in her post for long as she married the recently widowed head of the boys' school in July 1875, becoming stepmother to his infant daughter. However, she continued her involvement in education, writing up the school log on her husband's behalf and supporting his work in the NUT when they later moved to Great Harwood, Blackburn – as well as raising four children of her own.

On the other hand, Louisa remained a spinster, devoting her life to her teaching career. In 1879, she became headmistress of Almondbury Infants' school in Huddersfield at a salary of £80 per year. Seven years later she transferred to Mount Pleasant Infants' school as headmistress, this time on a salary of £115. There she remained in post for thirty-two years, until her retirement aged 65 in summer 1919.

Wakefield Council meeting minutes provide details of teachers appointed and their salaries and any increases agreed by the education committee. In 1906, they reveal a gender pay gap of seventeen per cent for the starting salaries of non-certificated elementary teachers, with male teachers receiving £60 a year and their female counterparts paid £50 for the same role. Their wages increased by increments of £2 10s every year. Certificated teachers received higher rates, starting at £65 for women and rising by annual increments of £5.

The newly appointed headmistress of St Austin's RC infants' school, Miss R. Weldon, was paid £90 per year, but longer-established headmistresses were earning higher salaries and receiving annual increases. Miss M.E. Hall, head of Holy Trinity National School (Girls) was paid £115, Miss K. Norman of Mr Gaskell's Girls' School at Thornes, £102 4s per year and Miss Gertrude Zillah Peaker, headmistress at the Cathedral (All Saints') Girls' School on Zetland Street, received £110 for her work. Miss Peaker was the daughter of Thomas, a carpenter and wagon builder and in 1911 was living with her father and sister at 1, Westfield View. Although she was still in her post as headmistress in 1927, the role may have been a strain, as she was admitted to the West Riding Asylum at Wadsley, Sheffield in February 1908, where she received treatment for four months before recovering. She passed away in a Scarborough Nursing Home in 1938, aged 62.

By the first decade of the twentieth century, pupil teachers were being engaged on two-year apprenticeships, where they spent time in the classroom, supported by study at the pupil-teacher centre at the technical college. The 1906 pupil teacher apprentices (all aged around 16) included:[16]

- Lucy Thornhill Cockell, at St John's Church School. Lucy was the daughter of Joe Cockell, an engine driver. She remained single, living at 76, Castleford Road, Normanton all her life and was still an elementary school teacher thirty-three years later, at the time of the 1939 register.
- Miranda Abson at Alverthorpe Council School. Daughter of Israel Abson, an iron-foundry manager, Miranda qualified as a teacher but married John Roberts, an engineer, in November 1916. Even though she was a qualified teacher, her wedding certificate gives no occupation.
- Evelyn Selley, at the junior mixed department of Eastmoor Council School. Daughter of a butcher of 16, Clarendon Street, Evelyn remained at home and was an assistant elementary school teacher at the time of the 1939 register, still living in the same house.
- Lucy Dearlove, at Ings Road Council School, lived at 24, Benjamin Street, Alverthorpe, daughter of a stonemason. Lucy married an engine driver, Albert Boyman, in 1923, and again her occupation as a teacher was not recorded on the marriage certificate.
- Mary Lucy Dews at Westgate Infants. Mary was the daughter of an engine tenter and lived at Lawefield Lane in 1911.

These were daughters of ordinary men, girls born without privilege into ordinary working families, for whom having an education meant they could train for a career, rather than just a job.

Even for well-educated girls, career opportunities were limited. Teaching provided not only material rewards but also professional status, and encouraged by their headmistresses and mothers, many girls chose this secure career. In the first decade of the twentieth century, elementary teaching was the largest single employment for girls leaving secondary school.

When the Burnham Committee put forward its proposals to introduce a uniform scale for teaching salaries, commencing with staff at elementary schools in 1918, there was an opportunity to bring women's pay to the same level as the men's. However, certificated male teachers with two years of college training received starting salaries of £160, increasing by annual increments of £10 to a maximum £300, whereas female teachers with the same qualifications started at £150, rising to £240. Head teachers were paid according to school attendance numbers, ranging from a grade 1 headmaster paid £330 to a grade 5 headmaster earning £450. Headmistress equivalents were paid £264 and £360 respectively.

Secondary school teachers received higher salaries, with graduate assistant masters paid £240 rising in £15 increments to £500 and graduate assistant mistresses £225 increasing by £12 10s annually to £400. Heads received £600 (men) and £500 (women).

It was a welcome pay increase for teachers in most local education authorities, and even though women were still paid lower wages than their male counterparts, the differential wasn't as marked as in clerical work or nursing, where women's wages were around seventy per cent, or less, of men's. It was a further thirty years before teachers had equality of pay. With no justification for this pay differential, understandably it rankled with women. They argued that, because men had far wider choice of occupation, male teachers were not drawn from the same academic elite as the women. If they were therefore of lower professional calibre, why should men be paid more?

Of course one counter-argument was that men had wives and families to support, whereas single women did not. There was indignation about women teachers being able to afford holidays abroad, while some men were having to take additional work, teaching night classes for example, to provide for their families. But what of the free housekeeping and care a man received from his stay-at-home wife? Did not women teachers have to pay someone to perform those duties for them?

At the annual meeting of the Association of Education Committees, a motion from Bootle near Liverpool, called for an early revision of the Burnham scale in view of the 'disproportionate and unwarranted salaries' paid to junior female teachers. It was argued:

> [T]o pay a young man £172 10s and a girl the same age and scale £160 was grossly unfair to the social system of the country. It was productive of late marriages instead of early ones, and leading the bachelor girl to position she ought not to occupy. The community which stood by and saw an expert ploughman, with his fifty-hour week, get a salary which did not exceed 40 shillings a week, including all perquisites, while his daughter got paid double that money for half the number of hours, was countenancing a state of things which was blot on the social life of the nation.
>
> *Yorkshire Post and Leeds Intelligencer*, 15 June 1923

It is quite telling that the status of a skilled ploughman was held in higher regard and worthy of higher pay than an educated woman who was training and influencing future generations.

Although guaranteeing current pay rates would remain until 1925, there was no doubt (in their minds) that the increased cost of education was caused by the increased salaries of women teachers so would require careful consideration at a later stage. Of course men's salaries had also increased but as women in the profession outnumbered men by 4 to 1, reducing women's wages would have more impact. There was to be no support given to the doctrine of equal pay for men and women.

Another justification for the lower pay and promotion opportunities for women was the notion that women would marry and leave teaching just at the time when their work was increasing in value. There was also anxiety in some quarters that women of a 'fine type' would eschew motherhood in favour of a career if they could be financially independent, so it was preferable to pay them lower wages. Even in 1940, the Royal

Commission on equal pay accepted the view that one of the social reasons for unequal pay was to make motherhood as financially attractive as paid work.

The stance on married women as teachers was reviewed annually by the West Riding Education Committee. It had been solemnly agreed with the NUT in 1922, that all married women in the profession before September of that year would not have their family circumstances enquired into, but in 1933 the staffing sub-committee proposed to break with the agreement. Citing the need to make room for young teachers coming out of college, the committee felt it wasn't right for married women to occupy the posts.

An amendment to refer the matter back was proposed by Mr A.J. Page of Knottingley (and seconded by Lady Mabel Smith, Labour councillor née Wentworth-Fitzwilliam). Unconvinced of a glut of teachers on the market, Mr Page rightly argued that until it was laid down that there should not be more than one income going into one house, action should not be taken against one particular profession.

However, as a similar rule applied to women working at the County Hall – any woman getting married had to resign her post – the committee decided if a married woman was in a pecuniary position to live without her teaching appointment she must give up her place. They believed it was perfectly sound policy to make it possible for young people, on whom public money had been spent on training, to come into the profession and the recommendation was adopted (*Yorkshire Post and Leeds Intelligencer*, 26 April 1933).

Outstanding talents

For many women who went into a profession it was another woman who inspired her to do so.

One influential woman, also inspired by another woman, was Gertrude McCroben, (born 10 March 1863 to a Bradford draper) who had studied at Bradford Girls' Grammar under its first headmistress, Mary Eliza Porter. Gertrude gained a scholarship to study mathematics at Newnham College, Cambridge in 1880. After qualifying, Gertrude became headmistress of Manchester Girls' Grammar School before being appointed headmistress at Wakefield Girls' High, taking over from Miss Allen in the summer of 1894. According to the newspaper announcement (*Bradford Daily Telegraph*, 10 July 1894) it was a position that carried with it considerable honour and emolument.

During Miss McCroben's twenty-five year tenure as headmistress, the number of girls attending the school increased from 139 to 542, making it one of the largest and best girls' schools in the country.[17] Gertrude was a firm believer in education for girls and campaigned for better organisation of curricula and the ways in which learning was tested. She was not in favour of cramming for exams. With regard to girls being taught the sciences (including her own subject of mathematics) Gertrude believed it trained the brain. This was especially necessary for girls, she said, 'who seem to be by nature lacking in logical sequence of ideas'. Parents and teachers were urged to unite to show children they should not merely drift through life, taking the path of least resistance:

> A good time was not the aim of life … children allowed to leave lessons undone to take part in pleasures would find it harder in later life when they leaned that work could not be just put to one side on a whim. Girls [and boys] who were allowed to give up learning subjects they found difficult were bound to become weak and inefficient people.
>
> *Leeds Mercury*, 29 September 1906

By the time war broke out in 1914, Miss McCroben had been in her post for twenty years. For women the war brought opportunities, but also frustrations and anxieties. Understanding everyone's sense of proportion had changed she urged others to live more worthily, in denial and with self-control and to face the challenges ahead.[18] In 1915, with many male teachers having enlisted, Gertrude spoke about the need for every woman and girl, who could do so, to offer her service to the teaching profession as an important form of war work. The shortage of elementary and secondary school teachers was a very serious problem, as without education, the next generation would suffer. The need for teachers was an urgent one if the country was to emerge from war 'a stronger nation, with higher ideals, greater capacities for energies, less inertness, and a more keen and trained intelligence' (*Leeds Mercury*, 4 December 1915).

Miss McCroben left the school in 1920, taking a position as a part-time inspector for a board of education in London. Later she worked as an examiner for the Joint Matriculation Board and continued until she was in her late-60s. She died on 25 July 1933 at her home in Lawn Crescent, close to Kew Gardens. Her financial legacy was divided into three, with her brother, sister and friend each receiving bequests, which upon their deaths passed to fund McCroben scholarships at Newnham and the school.

Five notable women who emerged from Miss McCroben's tutelage well-equipped for good careers, were the Lett sisters. Richard Alfred Lett, surgeon, and his wife, Bithiah (née Appleford) moved from Lincolnshire into 6, Southgate, in around 1886, with their two sons, Hugh and Richard, and four daughters – Norah Kathleen, Olive Mary, Phyllis and Hilda – and a private governess, Mary Eleanor Cobb. Another daughter, Eva, was born in Wakefield on 19 September 1887. After some home-tutoring all seven siblings were sent for formal schooling, the girls to Wakefield Girls' High.

By 1901, Norah had qualified as a school teacher and Olive had left home to train in dance and gymnastics.

Sadly their parents did not live to see their daughters prosper. Richard died on 19 December 1902, aged 55, from liver disease and meningitis, and Bithiah less than a year later, in her home county of Essex.

Phyllis and Hilda excelled in music, with Phyllis winning a free open scholarship in 1903, to study as a contralto singer at the Royal College of Music. Hilda trained at Leeds College of Music, before moving to further her studies as a violinist at the Guildhall School of Music in London, where in 1906 she was awarded the Tillie gold medal for the most distinguished lady violin student. Eva, the most academic, gained a place at Newnham College, Cambridge to study English and modern languages.

The most famous of the sisters was undoubtedly Phyllis, who became an internationally recognised contralto soloist, making her Royal Albert Hall debut on 1 November 1906, where she performed with the Royal Choral Society in their performance of Mendelssohn's *Elijah*. The review stated the newcomer had a 'contralto voice of pure character and much natural intelligence'.

Hilda was described in newspaper reports as a brilliant English violinist, and by 1907 had played several times before the royal family. The two sisters performed many times together, and were often welcomed back to Wakefield. By 1913, Hilda's career was beginning to be slightly overshadowed, and she was often introduced as 'the sister of the famous contralto'. Little wonder, since Phyllis's career was advancing to new heights. Among her many engagements she sang Elgar's *Sea Pictures* in a concert conducted by Sir Edward Elgar himself in October 1909 (the first of many performances with Elgar), and she was the principal contralto soloist in several of the Sir Henry Wood promenade concerts of the 1913 and 1914 seasons (at the time held at the Queen's Hall). Her association with Elgar stood her in good stead, when in March 1923 she brought a libel action against Pathé Frères Pathéphone Ltd. Pathé had recorded nineteen songs by Phyllis Lett in 1910, on a wax cylinder, and had released sixteen of them at the time of recording. The three unreleased songs were later issued, but not only had the original recording deteriorated during the preceding twelve years, the recording was not representative of Phyllis's more experienced voice. Her claim for damages was based on the fact that organisations wishing to engage her would buy these 'new' records, believing them to be a recent representation of her ability, and on hearing how awful her voice sounded, would not invite her to perform. She complained they had damaged her reputation.

In giving his evidence, Elgar described one of them as dreadful. In one place, what was really a long sustained note appeared on the record to be a dismal ululation. It was, he said, a wretched noise, one he did not recognise as representing any human voice. Another witness said he had to laugh because the voice was so raucous. On 10 April the case was settled by Pathé agreeing to destroy the three records and giving an undertaking that further reproductions would bear the date on which the songs were sung. The defendants also made a liberal contribution toward the costs of the case, so Phyllis was not out of pocket. She had achieved her objective and clearly Elgar still valued her as a soloist. In May 1924, she travelled to Paris with Leeds Choral Union for a concert tour in which Elgar would conduct his *Dream of Gerontius* and *Sea Pictures*. However, it was announced Phyllis would not be able to take part in a concert in Dieppe on the return journey. She had another very important engagement to prepare for – her marriage to Mr Charles Rupert de Burgh Ker MC on 7 June 1924, at St Margaret's, Westminster. Charles had served with the Australian army during the First World War, enlisting in August 1914, and taken part in the Gallipoli landings in April 1915. In June 1916, Second Lieutenant de Burgh Ker was awarded the Military Cross for conspicuous gallantry in removing ammunition from a wagon hit by enemy fire, but in November the same year he received gunshot wounds to his legs and chest, which eventually led to his discharge.

Phyllis's last London concert took place at the Queen's Hall on Friday, 13 March 1925, a farewell concert before emigrating to Australia with her husband later in the year – shortly after she'd recorded some performances with a different company – His Masters' Voice (HMV).

While Phyllis and Hilda were carving-out their musical careers, Eva was quietly progressing along a different path, influencing the lives of other women. After graduating from Cambridge she gained a teaching diploma and became a lecturer at St Hilda's College, Durham. From there she became vice-principal of Dudley Training College until 1921, then principal of the Physical Training College, Dartford – a women-only college founded by Swedish-born, physical education instructor and women's suffrage advocate, Martina Sofia Helena Bergman-Österberg.

In 1930, Eva was appointed principal of Ripon Diocesan Women's Teacher Training College, the first woman to hold the post. She remained there until August 1945, when she was compelled to retire through ill-health. In addition to her role as college principal, Eva had held offices at both the Ripon Diocesan Conference and Diocesan Education Council, been vice-president of the Ling Association (a PE association founded by a group of Dartford College graduates in 1899), and had been a member of the Board of Administration for Yorkshire Training Colleges, governor of Skellfield School for girls, manager of Ripon Holy Trinity Day Schools, a governor of Ripon Modern School, and president of the Ripon Business and Professional Women's Club. She passed away in a nursing home in Winchester on 30 November 1945, aged only 58. In tribute to her life, the Bishop of Ripon, Dr G.C.L. Lunt, said at her Winchester funeral:

> Under her leadership the training college has gone from strength to strength, and in her last two terms as principal she was seeing a vision for future developments and busily working out detailed plans for bold future policy, though she knew full well that it would not be hers to see these plans take material shape. It was by a miracle of superb courage that she remained at her post all through last term, carrying on her work with her usual patience and thoroughness, giving her best to staff and students alike, too deeply concerned about their well-being to have any leisure for thought of herself. Her own unswerving loyalty to her charge and to Him from whom she received it drew out from staff and students alike a fine and abiding loyalty and has enhanced and deepened the traditions of the college and made of it a fellowship which those who have received

their training here continue to value all their lives. She had strong reserve and did not easily make a multitude of friendships, but those whose privilege it was to work with her year by year came to realise the richness and depth of friendship which were hers to give. A deep spirituality and an inspiring self-discipline were balanced by a subtle and fragrant sense of humour. The name is legion today to those who as teachers or home-makers in every part of the country are conscious that their lives are forever the richer for the influence of her life upon theirs. She brought great gifts to her life work, but the greatest gift of all was herself, and that she freely gave.

The Yorkshire Post and Leeds Intelligencer, 4 December 1945

Eva wasn't the only Lett sister with an interest in women's physical education. Olive Mary Lett, born in 1882, trained as a gymnastics teacher and by 1909 was working in London. Her involvement in a display of girls' gymnastics at the Claremont Mission (a boys' and girls' club in Islington) was highly praised and she was also mentioned in *The Era* newspaper in connection with a 1910 performance in aid of a suffrage workshop, in which she had trained some Morris dancers. In the 1911 census taken 2 April, her occupation was listed as 'teacher of Swedish gymnastics'. Head of the two-person household at 70, Albany Mansions, Battersea Park was Helen Charlotte Elizabeth Douglas Ogston, whose occupation was 'organiser for women's suffrage society'.

This modest title belies the extent of Helen Ogston's involvement in the women's suffrage movement. In November 1908, Helen accompanied Sylvia Pankhurst and Flora Drummond to a meeting in Chelmsford, where she gave a speech to a rowdy crowd of hecklers at the Corn Exchange. By December 1908 she had achieved notoriety. Depicted on the front cover of the *Illustrated London News*, brandishing a dog whip as men push and jostle her, Helen Ogston became known as the 'woman with the whip'.

The *Aberdeen Press and Journal*, Monday, 7 December 1908, described the wild scenes of great disorder at the Royal

Albert Hall, caused by a woman's suffrage demonstration. Mr Lloyd George was addressing the gathered crowd of 9,000, but despite the verbal and written appeals to give him a fair hearing, the militant suffragettes representing the Women's Social and Political Union (WSPU) carried on a persistent course of disorderly conduct, threatening to completely wreck the meeting.

Lloyd George had hardly begun his speech when a tall young woman wearing a long maroon cloak, gesticulating theatrically, exclaimed in a deep ringing voice, 'Mr Lloyd George, what we want is deeds, not words.' Stewards immediately tried to seize her, but according to newspaper reports, she brought out a dog whip from beneath her cloak and lashed savagely at the first man who approached. Other men tried to carry her out by force. She was chained to her chair and 'her stinging lashes fell like a shower on their heads'. The Albert Hall was in tumult and there was a sustained scuffle before she could be removed.

The suffragettes in the hall continued their cries of 'deeds not words', and as one was ejected, another started up. The situation continued to deteriorate as 'the lunacy became worse' but Lloyd George pressed on despite the vitriolic onslaughts. It took him two hours to complete his prepared speech.

Sylvia Pankhurst's account of the incident in her book, *The Suffragette: The History of the Women's Militant Suffrage Movement,* tells that no sooner had Helen uttered her first words than a man in the next box leapt over the barrier and struck her in the chest, while stewards sprang her from behind. Another man stuck his lighted cigar into her wrist. Although she protested she would leave the hall at once, she was ignored, and used her dog whip in self-defence. Helen wrote to the newspapers to explain that having previously been subjected to serious violence and disgracefully mauled, she carried the dog whip as a measure against this happening again. She had, she said, in common with other members of the Women's Social and Political Union, the strongest natural repugnance to violence, but felt it her duty, in this instance, to make a protest against the sort of treatment to which no woman ought to submit. Undeterred from the cause, Helen continued to work hard with the Pankhursts and other leading suffragettes, and was described as an eloquent and persuasive speaker. There is no record of Olive Lett attending or speaking at these rallies, but it is likely she had some sympathies and connections with the cause. It would be hard to ignore in such a close friendship as she and Helen Ogston undoubtedly had – demonstrated by Olive's role as one of the two bridesmaids when Helen married Dr Eugene Dunbar Townroe on 4 May 1912 in Aberdeen – the other bridesmaid being Helen's sister, Constance.

Olive Lett's career in physical education continued at the Chelsea Training College, where she trained other women to become gymnastics instructors. These women were considered among the elite in their field and in huge demand as professional teachers in girls' schools.[19] In 1920, following a surge in popularity in folk-dancing, she was engaged to run a three-month programme of dance classes in Nottinghamshire, which culminated in a competition in Nottingham in December 1920.[20] The classes proved extremely popular and were recommenced the following February. Her key role in the English Folk Dance Society made her a valued adjudicator in folk-dancing competitions up and down the country, although like her sister Hilda, she was often introduced as the sister of the famous contralto.

In March 1933, aged 51, she married a widower, retired Major A.C.W. Cranko of Wootton Bassett and settled in Lower Eype in Dorset. Unlike many married women on the 1939 register, who give their occupation as 'unpaid domestic duties' she states she is living on private means. Perhaps a further nod to her independence and involvement in women's suffrage.

Wakefield's first female police officers

As well as campaigning for the right for equal pay and a right to vote, women also campaigned for equal workplace opportunities in positions traditionally occupied only by men.

The roles of women in the police force, as something other than clerical support, came under discussion when a deputation to Mr Ellis-Griffiths, under-secretary of state at the Home Office, pressed for the appointment of police women in July 1914.

Arguing that since women had already been appointed as factory and sanitary inspectors and that it was a natural progression to introduce women into police forces, the deputation believed the 'experiment of appointing women police could be safely undertaken, with the duties of police women clearly defined, and with the full and complete status of police officers'. Their work would have many benefits. They could give advice to women on the streets, which male constables were not in a position to give, and they could protect women from annoyance in cases where a man could not do so. Then they could, and ought to, take the statements of women and children in all cases involving immorality and be on duty at police stations when charges of offences against women and children were taken. And 'since every additional open space seemed to be an additional danger to children and girls who went there for enjoyment, the presence of police women would make very much for the improvement and safety of parks making them places of decent enjoyment for those for whom they were primarily intended'.

A second deputation, by Nottingham MP, Lord Henry Cavendish-Bentinck, asked that every police authority and watch committee should have two women constables in the force. But although Ellis-Griffiths agreed the welfare of women and children was the welfare of the community as a whole, he seemed reluctant to push legislation forward, saying it was exceedingly difficult to insist police authorities throughout the country should of necessity appoint women constables. There were no women who had taken the constable's oath or had the power of arrest, and there were already prejudices against women that might make county authorities and watch committees hesitant. He added (weakly):

It is a very moot point and a difficult one in law as to whether women can be appointed constables at the present time. I think the more strongly expressed opinion is that they cannot, and this matter you must carefully take into consideration. If it be so, you must legislate, and legislation is not easy in these days.

The chief constable of Leeds was in agreement with Lord Cavendish-Bentinck's desire to employ female constables for the special purpose of reformatory and preventive work and had discussed it with the chief constable of Liverpool. They agreed 'there are many delicate matters in which a woman well-trained in her duties, and of a shrewd and tactful disposition, would be inestimably preferable to a man.' Thinking a distinctive uniform would make women conspicuous and potentially the subject of ill-natured comment, they added, 'Should women police be appointed it would be as well to empower them to arrest, and in that case it would be necessary to distinguish them by a badge' (*Yorkshire Evening Post*, 22 May 1914).

Despite seeming willingness in some quarters to have women police on patrol, nothing happened. The First World War broke out and women were engaged to help in the police forces, but in what were essentially civilian roles. Volunteer special patrols of women 'police' worked in London to watch over the influx of women and girls hanging around army barracks, recruiting offices, and railway stations.

Late in 1918, the first women of the Metropolitan Police began training and in early 1919 were patrolling the streets as an experiment. It wasn't until 1923 that the first fifty women police were sworn in as constables of the Metropolitan Police and given powers of arrest.

Meanwhile the struggle to include women police in West Yorkshire continued. At a meeting of the West Riding Standing Joint Committee at Wakefield on 17 December 1924, the chief constable, Colonel Coke, referring to a communication regarding the employment of police women, said there was not sufficient work in the West Riding Constabulary to warrant their employment – and decided to take no action in the matter.

In January 1925, a deputation from the local branch of the National Council of Women visited the Bradford watch committee to urge the importance of including women constables in its city force, but it was reported in the *Common Cause*, 27 March 1925, that the watch committee had decided against employing women police for patrol duty. It did, however, propose that in cases of offences against women and children the evidence should be taken by suitably qualified women who would be classified as policewomen.

Despite persistent agitation from various groups, including the Women's Freedom League, a general reluctance to employ women as constables continued. With only eighty police women outside London a deputation (including Lady Astor) led by Ellen Wilkinson, MP for Middlesbrough, brought a Bill to the House of Commons under the ten minutes rule on 8 December 1925. It was an amending bill to the Municipal Corporations Act of 1882 – which allowed watch committee of borough councils to appoint sufficient numbers of fit men as police constables – and sought to impose a statutory duty for watch committees to appoint suitable women as constables also.

In a letter to the *Common Cause*, 11 December 1925, Ellen Wilkinson wrote:

> [S]ome may have been puzzled as to the reason why I am introducing a Bill in this particular form. There are several ways, of course, by which Watch Committees can be made to appoint women police. The Home Secretary has the power to issue regulations to this effect if he so desires, but it is unlikely that any Home Secretary of whatever party would care to face the hostility of reluctant Watch Committees without the backing of Parliament. This Bill gives the necessary support to the Home Secretary. It may also be argued that the Bill is unnecessary, as Watch Committees have the power to appoint women police and that the recent Home Office Committee even recommended them to do so. The plain fact is that most Watch Committees are reluctant, and that even if the Town Council is anxious for them to do so such a Council has no power to enforce its will. This was made unpleasantly clear last year at Manchester, when the City Council were informed that by an Order

made during the War, and still in force, they had no
power to discuss the minutes of the Watch Committee
which were only laid before them by courtesy for their
information! To no other Corporation Committee does
such a rule apply. The Bill is framed to deal with these
recalcitrant Watch Committees …

The Bill passed its first reading without opposition but was too
late in the parliamentary session to be progressed. Even when
pushed later, the Home Secretary, while in favour of women
police, was against compelling town councils to employ women
police. However, he did approve of an increase in the number
of women police in the Metropolitan Police Force, which was
directly under his control at the Home Office.

Campaigning for women to be employed as constables
continued. Some borough councils were more enlightened than
others. In February 1926, a meeting of the Leeds Society for
Equal Citizenship in Leeds heard that in Bolton, Lancashire,
despite the unfavourable attitude of the chief constable, they
had managed to get a woman police officer appointed, and now
had four with full powers of arrest. The speaker, Mrs Blincoe
(organising secretary of the Bolton Women's Citizenship
Association), told the meeting how those who had experience of
women police admitted they were very good and a commission
to investigate sexual offences strongly advised the appointment
of women police everywhere.

The West Riding Constabulary, with its headquarters in
Wakefield, also employed its first police woman in 1925, but
not, it seems, with the full powers of arrest. In January 1952, it
was reported[21] that Miss Mary Ethel Danby of Bradford Road,
Wakefield, had been promoted to chief inspector in the West
Riding Constabulary. At that time she had been a member of
the force for twenty-seven years, having started as a civilian
clerk in CID. She had been in charge of the Police Women's
branch of the constabulary since 1949, and was acknowledged
as the pioneer of women police in the West Riding. She was
also awarded the BEM in the New Year Honours that year. In
October the following year she was promoted to superintendent.

Mary's role cannot initially have been the same as her male colleagues as a report in the *Yorkshire Post and Leeds Intelligencer*, Thursday, 19 September 1940 reveals:

> Women Police in West Riding – at yesterday's meeting of the West Riding Standing Joint Committee at Wakefield a resolution proposed by Alderman W.M. Hyman that the Committee should accept the principle of employment of women for police patrol work was heavily defeated. An earlier recommendation that 50 members of the women's auxiliary police corps be employed whole-time on clerical work, telephone duties and motor drivers, was approved. It was stated by the Chief Constable (Mr. G. Campbell Vaughan) that on such work there was no need to give the women police powers. They would relieve for other duties men presently employed on such work. They would be engaged as required at rate of 40s per week, and uniforms could be provided.

Wakefield finally appointed its first police women to the city force in July 1942, following the appointment of Mr Alfred Godden as chief constable. Godden obtained approval from the watch committee in May to appoint twelve full-time members of the Women's Auxiliary Police Corps (WAPCs or 'Wapsies' as they were affectionately known).[22] The WAPC was one of the emergency forces set up during the Second World War and it was intended these women be employed on indoor roles, releasing men for street duties.

The terms and conditions stipulated they would not be special constables, nor be called upon to perform tasks requiring possession of police duties, but would render assistance to the police force in matters including:

1. Driving of motor vehicles.
2. Maintenance and repair of motor vehicles and other police equipment.
3. Clerical – including typing and shorthand.

4. Telephone and wireless work.

5. Canteen work.

Women had to be British subjects, aged between 18 and 55, mentally and physically fit. Their pay was fifty-two shillings a week (if over 20 years old) subject to deduction for national health and pension insurance and unemployment insurance, and with entitlement to disability and dependants' pensions and gratuities under scales approved for WAPC under the personal injuries (civilians) scheme of 1941. Uniform and equipment was provided – to be kept in good order and returned as such at end of the employment period – plus an allowance of 1s 6d weekly for boots.

The first two women, Freda Lambert WAPC1 and Grace Chester WAPC2 enrolled in early July 1942 – one as a typist, the other to work in the motor taxation office. They were also expected to tend to and search female prisoners when police matrons who usually did this work were off duty.

A week later they were joined by four other women, Myra Caines (née Griffiths), Marjorie Greenwood, Bessie Twentyman and Eva Davidson, and a further two – Irene Wainwright and Marjorie Williams – at the end of July. The women were mostly in their mid to late twenties and working in a clerical capacity for Wakefield companies, although Myra Caines was a qualified mental health nurse and Bessie Twentyman, a ladies' hairdresser. All, apart from Bessie, who left after only a short spell, stayed with the service till the WAPC was disbanded after the war.

In September 1942, the women were issued with uniforms of navy blue overalls bearing a circular badge embroidered with WAPC in pale blue. In May 1944, the Home Office authorised two of the Wakefield constabulary's WAPCs to carry out police duties. Freda Lambert and Marjorie Williams' roles didn't alter much, except they assisted CID in their investigations where women and children were involved and carried out occasional street patrols. Marjorie was commended for her work by the Wakefield magistrates in May 1945.[23]

Once the war was over and the WAPC disbanded, Wakefield City Police agreed to introduce two female police officers and three female civilian clerks to the force. On 1 April 1946, Miss Marjorie Williams was sworn in as Policewoman Constable 1 and on 29 April 1946, Miss Olive Winterbottom, aged 27, was appointed Policewoman Constable 2. Marjorie resigned on 21 July 1947, and Olive resigned in August 1948, probably as they were both to be married. Marjorie was replaced by Mavis Lee Holmes from Lupset who stayed in her post until January 1955. Kathleen Morgan, Olive's replacement, made a career as a police woman. She enrolled in Wakefield in November 1948, and transferred to Burnley in 1954 as a sergeant. Her progress continued back in Wakefield in 1961, before she moved again, via Barnsley to Brighton, where she was an inspector. She retired in Brighton in 1966 at the rank of superintendent.

Wakefield City Police did not increase its numbers of women police until 1959 (although it did appoint more men). In 1959 the force had ninety-six men and five women – four constables and one sergeant.

One interesting point was that although the women were paid less than their male colleagues, they were more generous. An unusual document in the West Yorkshire Archives reveals the donations in a collection made for a retiring superintendent. While the constables gave a shilling (some only sixpence) policewoman constable 1 gave 2s and policewoman constable 2 gave 1s 6d.

CHAPTER FIVE

The Health and Well-being of the Women of Wakefield

One long and widely held tenet was that of a woman's place being in the home. Although for most women there was little alternative than to marry and raise a family, even for those who were able to make home-making a conscious choice it wasn't an easy option. With maternal death rates at over 5 per 1,000 births, even in the 1930s, Wakefield MP Arthur Greenwood conjectured that motherhood was the most dangerous occupation, with the risks associated with giving birth higher than the perils faced by men who went down mines or to sea.

Between 1850 and 1890, married women made up around eighteen per cent of Wakefield's population (and married men another eighteen per cent). Widows and widowers accounted for a further six per cent. The percentage of married women (and men) in 1921 was slightly higher, with a higher percentage of widows – the impact of the First World War. There was also a tiny number of divorcees.

Marriage rates remained steady, with around two per cent of the population tying the knot every year. Just over a quarter of the women getting married during the period were under full age (21) compared with only nine per cent of men. Until the Marriage Act of 1929, which raised the legal marriage age to 16 for both sexes (with consent) children could marry (with parental consent) at the ages of 12 (girls) and 14 (boys).

Of course the higher proportion of women 'under full age' getting married with parental consent might be a reflection of the number of girls encouraged to marry their slightly older boyfriends in haste, before a baby arrived on the scene. Of the 1,644 babies born in 1850, 112 were born out of wedlock and this illegitimacy rate of seven per cent continued till the 1870s, after which there was a gradual reduction to around three per cent at the beginning of the twentieth century.

The number of women who were only able to sign the marriage register with 'her mark' gives some indication of education and literacy, and it is interesting to note that in 1850, almost fifty-seven per cent of women couldn't write their names, compared with thirty-five per cent of similarly illiterate men. But since most women were destined for a life of home duties, this may have been of little concern. However, by 1884, when the population had almost doubled and there had been improvements in education for both sexes, only seventeen per cent of men signed the register with a cross and twenty-five per cent of women.

Birth rates were higher in the mid-nineteenth century, with records showing the birth rate in the ten year period 1867–76 as 38.4 per 1,000 population. This gradually reduced to 23 per 1,000 in the decade 1907–16, and still further during the period of the First World War, when the rate was around 17 per 1,000. A post-war boom saw this rate increase to more than 26 per 1,000.[24]

The decline in birth rate concerned Wakefield's Medical Officer of Health, Dr Thomas Gibson, who cited the Registrar General in his 1905 annual report. National statistics showed there had been a general reduction in the numbers of babies born for some time, attributed to couples postponing marriage till they were at full age – thus reducing the childbearing period – and a decline in the number of illegitimate births. Dr Gibson went on to comment on the common observation that families were smaller, particularly among the well-to-do and the more provident and better-paid artisan classes. However, 'the fecundity of the impoverished and careless slum-dweller shows little sign of diminution'.

As Dr Gibson acknowledged, there was little he could do to increase the birth rate, but there was much that could and should be done to keep the babies that were born, alive and in good health.

Mother and baby healthcare

Sadly, the mothers of Wakefield experienced higher infant mortality rates than their peers in other parts of the country. For every 1,000 babies born in Wakefield between 1870 and 1879, 171 died before they reached their first birthday. This was almost fifteen per cent higher than average and it was five decades before any real improvements were made and Wakefield infant death rates were finally below the national average. The main causes of infant death were premature births, atrophy and debility and lung infections, such as pneumonia and bronchitis, with the majority occurring in working-class homes in congested districts. Mortality rates for illegitimate babies were twice that of babies born to married couples.[25]

Concerned by these statistics, a number of citizens established a voluntary organisation, the Wakefield Sanitary Aid Society, in January 1899. Its purpose was to tackle the population's lack of knowledge about sanitation and improve the public health of the city. The committee of men, presided over by the Bishop of Wakefield, first turned its attention to housing provision, employing an inspector to examine the poor circumstances in which people were living. At the time at least a quarter of Wakefield's population resided in old, crumbling houses, without through ventilation, often ill-lit and generally damp and lacking in amenities such as running water. Yards were largely unpaved, and typically of many West Riding industrial towns, toilet facilities consisted of dry privies located in rows of small outhouses. These used household ash to deodorise the smell. The alternative was the tub closet, basically a bucket 'tub' beneath a toilet seat, which required regular emptying. Many families in the city relied on common standpipes for their water supply and those in outlying districts obtained water from wells. But with the corporation unwilling to do much to improve housing and the sanitary committee reluctant to close a house unless it was on the verge of collapse, the pace of housing improvement was slow. Sometimes houses condemned by Dr Gibson were simply patched up and the corporation allowed their reoccupation. It took over thirty years to properly resolve Wakefield's appalling housing situation.

In 1900, with the infant mortality level reaching 200 per 1,000 – one in every five babies dying before its first birthday – an alternative approach was required, which required a woman's touch.

At the Sanitary Aid Society's annual general meeting in April 1902, it was proposed to appoint a lady inspector to attend to the sanitary work and 'get into friendly touch with the working women'. As part of the 'sanitary crusade' a systematic house-to-house inspection was advocated, in order to get public opinion sufficiently aroused to give the society the support it needed to carry out necessary reforms.

If they could get the people to understand that health was preferable to disease, that premature death was not a satisfactory thing – if they could only drill that, little by little, into the minds of their fellow creatures they would be doing great deal indeed (*Yorkshire Post and Leeds Intelligencer*, 22 April 1902).

The appointment took some time, but in 1903, the Sanitary Aid Society appointed its first health visitor, Miss Marguerite de Flemyng Boileau. Born in London on 3 January 1875, Miss Boileau was the daughter of a retired major general of the Bengal Staff Corps. Both her parents were Irish and her grandmother had been matron at the Westminster House of Correction (1851 census). Educated at Brighton High School, she had matriculated with a BA and a qualification in sanitary inspection from the University of London in 1894, through private study and tuition. Her arrival in Wakefield heralded a turning point in the health of babies and their mothers. She was a well-qualified expert in the observance of sanitary law in the homes of the working classes and carried out her pioneering work with enthusiasm and tact. It made her hugely appreciated for her advice by the mothers in the slums and widely respected by the city council to whom she relayed valuable information concerning the lives and habits of the local 'submerged tenth'.

Her main work involved educating mothers, but before advising specific measures she wisely availed herself of the facts by visiting them in their homes and learning about their practices. In her first 2½ years she made 6,000 visits to 900 babies. What she gleaned was that although poverty was responsible for some infant mortality, it was not the sole cause. Wakefield was free of some of the issues affecting infant health in other towns. Mothers were not employed in mills, there were no markedly unhealthy occupations and none of the home work trades prevalent in large cities. Drunken mothers were rare – although there were drunken fathers whose habits deprived their families of adequate nourishment – and a large proportion of babies were breast-fed.

Miss Boileau asserted the main culprit in Wakefield's high infant mortality rate was 'crass ignorance combined with devoted affection'. Many mothers believed the only reason their babies were crying was through hunger and she found many babies being fed two or three times an hour and given soothing syrup at night to help them sleep. In four out of five cases, babies screaming with pain from overfeeding were fed again. Even mothers with healthy plump babies were convinced their milk was not satiating and were weaning them onto solid food, usually bread sops and biscuit. It was a lot to combat, and required great patience and tact to persuade mothers to lengthen the intervals between feeding, and to make them realise the harm wrought in drugging babies to sleep.

Although tactful to mothers, she wasn't reticent in stating her views to other officials, and these were reported nationally.

> Probably every sanitary inspector and health visitor comes into frequent contact with the prejudices and superstitions of those venerable dames who regard it as their mission in life to oppose what they term the

'new-fangled' ideas of the present generation. But very few officials would have the courage of Miss Boileau, of the Wakefield Sanitary Aid Society, who in set terms denounces grandmothers as a 'terrible stumbling-block' to progress. They (the grandmothers) urge the efficacy of gin and soothing syrup, and two large doses of castor oil per week 'to keep away fits'. In one case Miss Boileau found a 4-day-old baby being given tomato while a 14-day-old was being fed with gruel and arrowroot biscuits. Other babies had been given tea, pancake, soup, rhubarb pie, etc. But despite these illustrations of ignorance and stupidity, Miss Boileau may take comfort that some advance is being made, though it is far slower than could be wished.

Ardrossan and Saltcoats Herald, 11 January 1907

Poor housing conditions were another area to be tackled. In her report to the Sanitary Aid Society in November 1905, Miss Boileau revealed the still lamentable standard of Wakefield's housing, particularly in bedroom accommodation, and lack of water supply. There were still 475 houses in Wakefield without water taps or sinks and, in all weathers, women had to carry buckets of water from taps some distance from their homes. Disposing of dirty water down the nearest grating was no fit task for a mother and many women were injured, sometimes permanently, in the process.

And while she understood the difficulties of overcrowding where one man's wage had to provide for a wife and several school-age children, Miss Boileau could see no reason why, once the children became wage-earners, families could not rent larger houses. She called on teachers, district visitors, and others with influence over working-class mothers, to emphasise the evils of sleeping in overcrowded bedrooms and point out, where possible, their duty to devote part of the increased household income to renting larger homes.

One of Miss Boileau's main concerns was how unprepared mothers were for the arrival of babies. In 1906, she founded

Wakefield's 'Babies Welcome', a provident society which encouraged pregnant women to help themselves by saving a modest weekly amount so there was money to buy the necessities when their babies were born. It was the first such society in the country and Miss Boileau was supported by a team of Wakefield ladies, who helped to extend its activities to supply food and clothing and assist mothers in other ways. Her unstinting work began to pay off. Infant mortality rates began to reduce significantly, other towns took up her idea and founded Babies Welcome groups, and her work was highly commended in the *London Times*. Miss Boileau was regarded as one of the most efficient lady health visitors in the country.

In March 1907, the Sanitary Aid Society, with only sufficient funds to keep Miss Boileau for a further six months, approached Wakefield's council, proposing that it, like other corporations, should consider the desirability of incorporating the care of infants as a permanent department of municipal sanitary work. It suggested appointing 'some experienced lady visitor' as one of the recognised staff of its sanitary department. But the council declined to employ Miss Boileau at her £120 a year salary, stating it did not want to burden rate-payers with more expense. Arguing that the committee failed to realise the impact her work had on the health of the city's children, the mayor managed to get the matter referred for further consideration. However, in July 1907 it was reported that the city council had declined to make the appointment. The action was seen as extraordinary, and many suggested it was due to jealousy. After all, in significantly reducing infant mortality, Miss Boileau had accomplished in three years what the men on the city council had failed to achieve over decades. A successful appeal was launched for subscriptions to enable the Sanitary Aid Society to keep her services, and her work continued.

In late 1908, when the Sanitary Aid Society disbanded, the council was finally persuaded to engage Miss Boileau as an 'unofficial' lady health visitor, to work under the direction of the medical health officer, on condition her salary was provided for two years by certain public-spirited ladies interested in her

Wakefield's Market Cross with the cathedral in the background. The cross, built in 1707 was used for public meetings and for the sale of eggs, butter and poultry, but demolished in 1866, despite public protest. The image is a black and white copy of a painting is by Louisa Fennell, a talented watercolour artist, whose portfolio included many images of Victorian Wakefield. (Wakefield Council Libraries. Photographic Collection)

Wives and daughters of important men of the city were invited to lay foundation stones when St John's Church underwent extensive renovations in 1885. Note they are identified by their relationships to the men.

Emma Moorhouse. Wife of George Moorhouse, Mayor.

Above: *Charlotte Matilda Bell. Wife of Edward Bell MA, Vicar.*

Below: *Edith Grace Mackie. Daughter of Robert Bownas Mackie, MP. Two months later he was dead.*

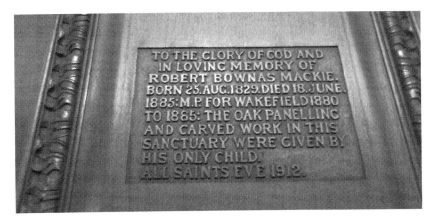

THIS STONE WAS LAID
BY EDITH G. MACKIE
IN WORSHIP OF GOD
12 OCTOBER 1904

Twenty years later, without husband or father to exercise control, Edith used her wealth to support to the church and was invited to lay another foundation stone.

TO THE GLORY OF GOD AND
IN LOVING MEMORY OF
ROBERT BOWNAS MACKIE,
BORN 25.AUG.1829.DIED 18.JUNE.
1885:M.P FOR WAKEFIELD 1880
TO 1885: THE OAK PANELLING
AND CARVED WORK IN THIS
SANCTUARY WERE GIVEN BY
HIS ONLY CHILD:
ALL SAINTS EVE 1912.

Above: *Edith Mackie's ongoing benevolence to St John's is demonstrated in this panelling.*

Right: *Edith Grace Mackie.* (Courtesy of St John's Church, Wakefield)

Above: *St John's House, inherited by Edith Grace Mackie upon the death of her father in 1885. She continued to live in the house until 1934, when she moved to a smaller (27-room) 'cottage' called Amberd on Blenheim Rd. St John's House was opened as Wakefield Girls' High School Junior Department in January 1967.* (Wakefield Council Libraries Photographic Collection. Courtesy of Mr E. Raper)

Below left: *Miss Ellen Allen, Wakefield Girls' High School first headmistress from 1878-94.* (Courtesy of the Wakefield Grammar School Foundation Archives)

Below right: *Gertrude McCroben, Wakefield Girls' High School second headmistress from 1894-1920.* (Courtesy of the Wakefield Grammar School Foundation Archives)

Wakefield Girls' High School Science Laboratory, installed in 1905. (Courtesy of the Wakefield Grammar School Foundation Archives)

Wakefield Girls' High School Library in 1910. (Courtesy of the Wakefield Grammar School Foundation Archives)

A class of girls at Ings Road School, where Lucy Dearlove started her teaching career in 1906. The photo is dated 1905-15. (Wakefield Council)

Sugden's Workwear Factory.
(Courtesy of The Double Two
and Sugden's Companies)

*Women and girls
filling shells by hand
at E. Green and Sons,
Calder Vale Road. 1914-18.*
(Wakefield Council)

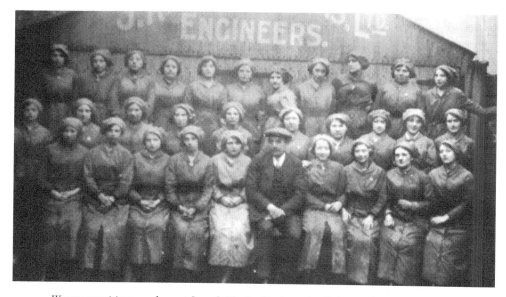

*Women munitions workers at Joseph Rhodes Engineering Ltd on Elm Tree Street, Belle
Vue, during the First World War.* (Wakefield Council Libraries Photographic Collection)

Above: *Local women in the Land Army during the Second World War.* (Wakefield Council)

Below: *Betty Amy Wandless, born Altofts in 1923, and living in Wakefield in 1939 served in the WAAF from January 1943 to autumn 1946. Her reference on leaving:*

"The above named airwoman is a willing and reliable worker of excellent character. She has been employed as a batwoman and has recently been in charge of a WAAF hairdressing shop where she has given valuable service. She is recommended for employment as a hairdresser having had three years' experience in this profession prior to joining the service. (Courtesy of Claire Crossdale)

Above: *'This is just how fast we can sew'. Women show off their skills on Double Two Shirts' stand at the British Industries Fair 1948.* (Courtesy of The Double Two and Sugden's Companies)

Left: *Double Two Shirts' employees pressing and Ironing on Exhibition Stand at the British Industries Fair 1948.* (Courtesy of The Double Two and Sugden's Companies)

Sugden's Production Area 1950s. (Courtesy of The Double Two and Sugden's Companies)

Above left: *Florence Beaumont presented to court c. 1910.* (Courtesy of the Beaumont family)

Above right: *Florence Beaumont and her dachshund named after 19th century women's suffrage campaigner John Stuart Mill.* (Courtesy of the Beaumont family)

Right: *Phyllis Lett, world famous contralto.* (Courtesy of the Wakefield Grammar School Foundation Archives)

Left: *6, South Parade, Wakefield, the home of the Lett sisters from 1886 to 1900.* (Wakefield Council Libraries Photographic Collection. Courtesy of Mr John Goodchild M Univ)

Below: *St John's Auxiliary Military Hospital at Wentworth House, the premises of Wakefield Girls' High School.* (Courtesy of the Wakefield Grammar School Foundation Archives)

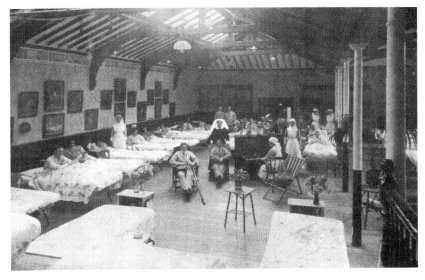

Above: *Wellington Ward St John's Auxiliary Military Hospital at Wentworth House. Notice the nurse playing the piano to entertain the patients.* (Courtesy of the Wakefield Grammar School Foundation Archives)

Below: *An invitation card from the Ladies Committee of the annual Wakefield Charity Ball, which raised funds for Clayton Hospital.* (Wakefield Council Libraries Photographic Collection)

The Ladies Committee of the Wakefield Charity Ball
request the pleasure of the company of

at the Annual Ball
to be held in the Corn Exchange, Wakefield,
on Wednesday, January 4th 1899
In aid of the funds of the Clayton Hospital.

The favour of an early reply is requested, addressed to the Hon. Secretary,
John W. Walker,
The Elms,
Dancing at 9 o'Clock.
Wakefield.

Tickets 12/6 each may be had after January 1st of Mr W. H. Milnes, Market Place

Above: *Clayton Hospital opened on 30 July 1879, although the original had been established in 1854. As well as healthcare it provided training and employment for countless women of Wakefield.* (Wakefield Council Libraries Photographic Collection. Courtesy of Mr R. G. Pearson)

Below: *Betty Amy Wandless, bottom left in white overalls with her hairdressing kit at Pinderfields Hospital June 1951.* (Courtesy of Claire Crossdale)

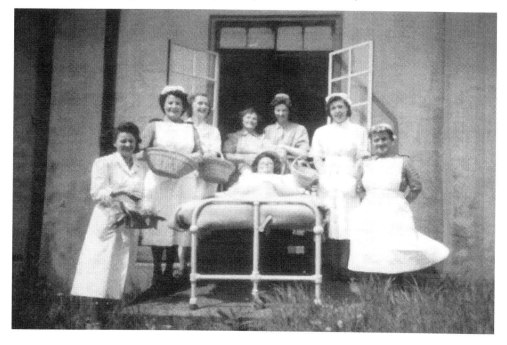

Women teachers at Alverthorpe County Infants School 1948. (Wakefield Council Libraries Photographic Collection. Courtesy of Mrs J. Wilkinson)

Lady Kathleen and Mary Pilkington at Newmillerdam. Note Mary's woven basket, probably for collecting soft fruits. (Courtesy Elsie Walton)

Mrs Ellen (Nellie) King née Hartwell, head mistress at St John's Infants' School 1882-1895 and Clarendon Street Infants' from 1895. Commandant Clayton VAD and St John's Auxiliary Military Hospitals Wakefield from August 1914 to February 1919. Awarded Royal Red Cross 2nd Class. (Courtesy of St John's Church, Wakefield)

Above: *Gwendoline Beaumont, the first woman from Wakefield to stand for parliament.* (Courtesy of the Beaumont family)

Left: *Lady Catherine Milnes Gaskell, pictured around 1889.* (Wakefield Council)

Below: *Thornes House, Thornes, Home of Catherine Milnes-Gaskell until 1919. It became Thornes House School in 1921.* (Wakefield Council Libraries Photographic Collection. Courtesy of Mr P. I. Wood)

THORNES HOUSE

Above: *Houses at Duncan Yard, off Thornes Lane, in the 1930s just prior to the 'slum clearance'.* (Wakefield Council Libraries Photographic Collection)

Below: *Tenants with Mrs Effie Crowe (Wakefield's second female mayor) and her mayoress outside their new council house in 1945.* (Wakefield Council)

Above: *VE Day celebrations on the Portobello estate.* (Courtesy of Mrs Hazel Beevers)

Below: *Ladies' Day Trip from Flying Horse public house 1950. One wonders how the two male coach drivers coped!* (Courtesy of Denise Green)

work. These ladies were led by Mrs Anna Louisa Milnes-Gaskell of Lupset Hall, widow of Gerald Milnes-Gaskell and sister-in-law of Lady Catherine Milnes-Gaskell of Thornes House.

Another 'official' lady health visitor was appointed to work alongside Miss Boileau, but her work included working as the school nurse – a new role. Noting that summer diarrhoea, a disease that carried off a great number of babies every year, was rarely apparent in breast-fed babies, and that rickets, another common disorder in Wakefield, caused much ill-health and deformities of the body, Wakefield's health department implemented a programme of education for mothers and mothers-to-be to encourage more breastfeeding and better hygiene. The council produced a leaflet to be circulated to all mothers, insisting they follow the directions contained therein to greatly increase the chance of their children growing up strong and healthy.

Taking note of Miss Boileau's findings, it advised:

The chief rules of infant feeding are as follows

1. Feed at the breast if possible. The mother's milk is a natural food and the best.

2. If the infant cannot be fed at the breast, feed on fresh cow's milk properly prepared.

3. Feed at regular intervals.

4. Do not use a long tube with a bottle – a boat-shaped bottle with a teat only is the best.

5. Keep bottle and teat scrupulously clean.

6. Keep dust and flies out of the milk.

7. On no account give the infant any food except milk until the teeth appear.

8. Wash the infant over every day.

9. Keep the house clean and let plenty of fresh air in.

10. Do not delay sending for the doctor if baby is ill.

Adding:

> in order that milk may be abundant and wholesome from
> the first, the mother should lead a regular life before
> baby is born, should take plenty of wholesome food,
> avoiding stimulants such as spirits and beer, and while
> taking plenty of exercise, should abstain from over-
> exertion. She should not take drugs except on the order
> of a doctor. If she has not been able to suckle previous
> children owing into a lack of milk she should consult
> a doctor early. Of course the mother must continue to
> attend most carefully to her own health during the time
> she is nursing.

When Miss Boileau left in 1910, she was replaced by a second official health visitor, and recognising the benefit these ladies were bringing, additional health visitors were appointed at intervals, and by 1929 there were six (see Appendix 5). However, instead of being totally devoted to maternity and child welfare, the ladies worked in their own specific districts, carrying out the additional duties connected with the school medical service, plus mental deficiency and TB. It meant only half their time was devoted to maternity and child welfare.

With staff unable to cope with the workload, once again volunteers were called upon to assist. A voluntary auxiliary service was set up to oversee certain infants selected by the health visitors. Twenty-four ladies enlisted and attended a special course of lectures at the town hall in order to better qualify themselves for their duties. They met monthly with the health visitors and medical officer, and it was during their discussions that the idea for arranging regular meetings for mothers and babies was raised. In 1912, with the support of these ladies, the first 'Mothers Club' meeting took place in the town hall on 15 April. Thirty-seven mothers attended. Fortnightly meetings continued and their success meant the club outgrew the capacity of the room and was moved to more commodious quarters at the Old Coffee Tavern in Upper Kirkgate in 1915.

At the same time two additional centres were opened – one at the Homestead in Alverthorpe Road and the other (which moved to the Primitive Methodists' Sunday School rooms in Doncaster Road the following year) at Haddingley Hill. A fourth centre was opened at the St John's mission room in Providence Street in 1916. This quiet, unpretending centre was deliberately sited in the middle of a poor locality, in the hope that the mothers 'who fought shy of going in their shawls' to other centres, would attend. The plan was a success. The fifth and sixth centres were opened in 1917 at Eastmoor and 1919 in Thornes Lane. As demand increased, centres were moved to accommodate the numbers attending and by 1920, the six child welfare centres were at Alverthorpe, Homestead, Market Street, Eastmoor, Thornes Lane and Belle Vue, where they remained for a further ten years.

In 1919, 545 mothers were registered at the child welfare centres, with 373 infants and 288 children aged between 1 and 5 years. On average they attended the clinics fifteen times a year. Sixty-three expectant mothers attended around seven times, probably in the last trimester of their pregnancies.

Statistics from the medical officer's report around the same period show that in one year the five lady health visitors – Sarah S. Thorp, Edith Greenwood, Ada Knox, Ellen R. Paver and Eliza E. Bell (all CMB (Central Midwives Board) certified) – made a total of 16,023 home visits (around thirteen per day), including 7,979 visits to infants and 557 to expectant mothers. On top of that there were 340 attendances at child welfare centres and 596 visits to schools, where they made 12,880 examinations for cleanliness and 468 for treatment. It was a huge workload for these women, but one that started to show results as mothers heeded their advice. In a five-year period between 1923 and 1928, the percentage of women breast-feeding their babies for six months or longer increased from sixty-eight per cent to eighty-three per cent, with a further 6.5 per cent breastfeeding for up to six months. This, combined with improved hygiene practices, helped reduce infant mortality, so that by 1930 it was half what it had been in 1905.

The Babies Welcome team was also intimately associated with the centres, assisting the paid professionals by making itself responsible for not only the supply of voluntary workers but also the supply of tea and other services to mothers. This productive union, between official and voluntary services, was strengthened by the appointment of representatives of the Babies Welcome team onto the Mental and Child Welfare committee of Wakefield Corporation in 1930. The committee's duties included overseeing the registration of nursing homes and the notification of births and its remit on maternity and child welfare involved the management of the maternity home and child welfare centres, plus child life protection. With only a handful of women on the council (of which three were appointed to the committee of thirteen) and the focus on women's issues it is noteworthy that other women were necessarily co-opted to help and advise with council work. These women were mainly married ladies in their forties and fifties, with grown-up families. Some had had careers prior to marriage, such as Elizabeth May Matilda Appleyard (née Abbey) who had been an elementary school teacher, and Alice Ann Martin (née Rollinson) who had been an assistant to a ladies outfitter. Others were wives of ordinary working men – railway guards, colliery surveyors – a contrast to some of the grander benevolent women of the city (see Appendix 4).

Once a principal child welfare centre was opened in Margaret Street in 1930, the Market Street, Eastmoor, Homestead and Thornes Lane centres all closed. Alverthorpe was replaced by a new centre at Snapethorpe Hall on the new Lupset housing estate in 1931, and on 12 November 1935, Belle Vue transferred to new child welfare premises adjoining the newly-built maternity hospital at Manygates Park.

Although all child-welfare centres were eventually held on corporation-owned premises, it was the kindness and philanthropy of various organisations who provided accommodation at nominal rents, inconvenience and possibly financial loss to themselves, which made a substantial contribution to helping mothers and the progress of child welfare in the city.

As well as infant and child welfare there was also a need for improvements to maternity provision. The maternal death rate was a cause for concern nationally, as despite reductions to the infant mortality rate and death rates in general, it remained at 5 per 1,000 live births. One reason cited was the fall in the birth rate was creating a higher proportion of first confinements, which involved more risk to mothers.

The Maternity and Child Welfare Act of 1918, empowered local councils with the authority to implement a wide range of measures to aid maternity services in their districts. These included the establishment of ante- and post-natal clinics, the appointment of municipal midwives, and financial assistance to private midwives to enable them to practise. Maternity homes or beds in a maternity hospital were to be provided for complicated cases, for patients whose circumstances were not suitable for home confinement, for ante-natal observation, or the treatment of puerperal sepsis. Of course this wasn't all free. Patients were expected to contribute towards the cost of special services according to their means.

A maternity ward existed in Wakefield's Poor Law Infirmary, but was mainly used for the confinement of unmarried women who perhaps had no homes of their own in which to give birth. Complicated cases were sometimes referred to Clayton Hospital, but there was no real provision for maternity care. In 1917, Dr Gibson submitted a scheme which was taken up by the Mental and Child Welfare Committee and in April 1919, Wakefield's first municipal maternity hospital admitted its first patient to the premises at St John's Mount, Blenheim Road. It marked a great advance and extension of the work for maternity and child welfare in the city. The matron, on a salary of £80, was Charlotte Dickson, from Great Ormond St Children's Hospital. There were just twelve beds, plus a further four for isolation cases. Fees for mothers were set at 10s per day, plus a further 2s for maintenance.

In its first year it admitted sixty-two patients, but the following year saw the number treble, although hospital births only represented fourteen per cent of all births in the city. In 1921, Miss Dickinson was succeeded as matron by Helena Joyce More, who stayed just two years before marrying physician Thomas Shand, the city's assistant medical officer in 1923. Edith Sarah Annie Morton was her successor.

Another facility to improve the health and well-being of expectant mothers was the ante-natal clinic, first established in the town hall in 1916. Held only once a month, it was not a great success, but improved once it transferred to the maternity hospital three years later. Weekly sessions were gradually increased to two and three a week to meet the growing demand, with a post-natal clinic added in 1928. That year also saw the appointment of Dr Jessie Eeles, who left her post as senior lady resident doctor at the Edinburgh maternity hospital, to take charge in Wakefield as assistant medical officer for maternity and child welfare. Her salary was £600.

Confinements in the maternity hospital gradually increased, reaching a high of 410 in 1931, and by November 1935, when the hospital transferred to the new nine-acre site at Manygates, 4,595 babies had been delivered in its wards.[26]

The new thirty-five bed maternity hospital, child welfare centre and ante-natal clinic at Manygates Park cost £27,000 and was officially opened by the mayor of Wakefield, Mr F.W.T. Mills on 10 October 1935. Mrs Effie Hirst Crowe, chairman of the Mental and Child Welfare Committee, who presided over the events, stated that in planning the new hospital the corporation had in mind the needs not only of Wakefield citizens but those of surrounding districts, for which Wakefield was a convenient centre. In his speech the mayor highlighted the combination of official and voluntary effort in Wakefield's maternity and child welfare work, citing the thirty years of voluntary work by the Babies Welcome group as being instrumental in reducing local infant mortality by two-thirds. However, the position regarding maternal mortality was not quite as satisfactory.

In his vote of thanks, local MP Arthur Greenwood reminded people that in spite of the fact the physique of children had been improved enormously and the death rate reduced in recent years, maternal mortality in Wakefield was still higher than in a lot of other towns. It was monstrous, he said, that in the twentieth century they seemed unable to reduce the loss of life resulting from what was a perfectly normal function. He believed it to be the ugliest social factor of the time (*Leeds Mercury,* 10 October 1935).

As well as having triple the number of beds, the new hospital had a much larger staff, headed by Dr Jessie Eeles, supported by Matron Kate Perkins – appointed in December 1931 – a deputy matron, a night sister, two day sisters, a nurse and six midwives (see Appendix 5).

Wakefield gained another maternity hospital in July 1942, when the West Riding council opened Walton Hall as an emergency maternity hospital for evacuees from the London blitz. The hall, situated on a small island in a large lake, was described in the *Yorkshire Post and Leeds Intelligencer* as 'one the strangest sites for a hospital of its kind in the country'. The only access to the building was over a narrow, arched footbridge, but it was believed to have one of the finest labour wards of any emergency home. It was also peaceful, restful and safe – a complete contrast to the situation in London – where Walton Hall's first matron, Miss O'Laverty, had been delivering babies in cellars during air-raids.

After the war, Walton continued as a maternity home until the 1960s. After one new mother threw her baby into the lake from the footbridge, new mothers were forbidden to carry their babies until a nurse had carried it off the premises and handed it to the mother.

One scheme to improve the health of expectant mothers was not taken up by many. On the grounds that bad teeth not only affected general health but could also lead to septic complications at childbirth, pregnant women were offered dental treatment, but with 1930s' dentistry techniques probably instilling fear into women, the scheme was not a success. Hoping more people would take advantage of it, a new dental clinic was provided alongside the ante-natal clinic on Manygates Lane in 1935. And in another effort to reduce maternal mortality rates, facilities for contraceptive treatment were also introduced. Whatever anyone's opinions were about contraception in general, it was agreed to be desirable and necessary to prevent pregnancies in married women for whom getting pregnant might cause health issues and potentially, death.

Support for debilitated mothers who had sustained difficult births came from both Babies Welcome and the Wakefield Rotary Club, who, from 1925, helped meet the cost of sending them to convalescent homes. Additional financial aid came from the corporation, when a Yorkshire home for mothers and babies was opened in Withernsea on the east Yorkshire coast in June 1931. It sounded just the ticket for new mothers:

HOLIDAY HOME FOR MOTHERS AND BABIES –
PERAMBULATOR SQUAD ON A SEASIDE PARADE

Standing in its own grounds of five acres and overlooking the North Sea, there is a house in the little seaside town of Withernsea which will restore the health of at least 120 mothers and their young babies this summer. The house is Hop Villa, which has been taken over by the Baby's Welfare Association in conjunction with others who are interested in the enterprise, and has been named the Yorkshire Home for Mothers and Babies. It was formally opened on Saturday, although a number of mothers have already enjoyed a holiday there. Here mothers forget the word housework for a fortnight because a stay at Hop Villa is essentially complete rest. Brushes, coal buckets, floor mops and cooking utensils are simply not mentioned during an all-too-short, but carefree stay in the home, where many mothers spend their first real holiday for years.

... If a visitor wants to see one of the mothers during the morning, afternoon or early evening, it is useless to go to the home for they will not be found there. One is more likely to see them walking along the sea front in a body and pushing their youngsters in the prams which are provided by the home. The mothers, who come from all parts of Yorkshire, but chiefly from the West Riding and Hull, have breakfast shortly after nine o'clock, and they can be seen on the front before ten o'clock. At 12.30 they return for lunch, are out again soon after two o'clock, and, having had tea, the babies are put to bed and the mothers go out again until about half-past eight.

The secret of the home's success is plenty of fresh air. It makes a great difference in the health of the mothers and the babies. The youngsters, in fact, seem to thrive beyond the highest hopes of Dr F. R. Cripps, who examines and weighs them several times week. So far only one baby has failed to put on weight during the fortnight. On the promenade I met some of the mothers who had only just arrived, and had seen comparatively little sunshine, yet they talked proudly about the bronzed appearance of their children. Inside the home everything suggests a quiet, restful holiday. No doubt the outside appearance of the building would not impress you, for it was formerly a farm house, substantial, with straight walls of grey brick. It might be mistaken for a large coastguard's house, but inside a different scene awaits one.

It is, in fact, a most comfortably furnished home, with only one rule. The rule, which is to be found hanging in the babies' bathroom, informs the mothers that they must not leave the tap running while the baby is in the miniature bath, and they must not leave a child alone for a single moment when it is being bathed. Life, indeed, could never be made simpler for any mother. When the babies are put to bed they are looked after by the matron, Miss E.J. Woollcombe, and the nurse, Miss Wise, while the mothers are out obtaining the full benefit of the sea air. And apparently Miss Woollcombe relishes her job, for, when I asked her what it was like to look after 12 babies at once, she smiled and told that it is either a soft job or a task, for if one baby starts crying the rest soon join in. This only happens, apparently, during the first one or two days, for soon as they have become acclimatised they settle down to healthy slumber.

At present, and until the money is forthcoming for the extension which the organisers propose to build on the five acres of land that are available, the number of mothers who are accommodated is 12. Friendships are rapidly made, and on the first night of the stay the gramophone is soon keeping everyone amused. Throughout the building the decorations have been carried out in green and lemon, a somewhat unusual scheme for a home of this description. But thereby hangs a tale. The matron, who has had extensive experience in the running of institutions ... does not like red, and wonders why many homes and institutions favour this colour. Miss Woollcombe's appointment at Hop Villa, however, gave her an opportunity to use her own ideas in the general decorative scheme and there can be no doubt that the departure from the accepted idea has been a success.

In addition to supplying ideas, Miss Woollcombe travelled 5,000 miles collecting the furnishings, which have been provided either by individuals or through subscription funds started in various places, including Leeds, Withernsea, Halifax, Rotherham, Wakefield, and Hull. For example, the day room furniture, including the easy chairs, was supplied by Leeds and the beds and bedding by other towns. Each bed is provided with a green cover in order to harmonise with the surroundings. Above everything else, however, the home is a place of rest for the mothers, who have their meals cooked by electricity, and when they return from their afternoon stroll, find a dainty tea waiting for them.

Dundee Evening Telegraph, Wednesday, 10 June 1931

A further home opened in Harrogate in 1935, and both mother and baby homes proved a blessing to several poor and weakly mothers. The facilities were shared with other Yorkshire towns and cities, so it must have been an interesting trip for the forty or so lucky Wakefield mothers who went each year.

Mothers and babies were also supported by a team of midwives. Before the 1902 Midwives Act, all Wakefield's midwives were untrained, but the act made it compulsory for midwives to be trained for three months and registered. A Central Midwives Board (CMB) was founded to agree the standards to which midwives must work. The training period for untrained women was extended to six months in 1916, though trained nurses could complete the course in four months. However, untrained but experienced midwives were able to continue their work and even in 1922, twenty years after the Act, eight out of the fourteen midwives who practised from their homes in Wakefield were untrained. There were a further four trained and certified midwives in the city – three at the maternity hospital and one at the Union Infirmary. Not all untrained midwives were negligent, but the coroner raised concerns about having to hold inquests on premature babies who had died without receiving medical attention and there were complaints from patients of some midwives refusing to visit them on Sundays. The city medical officer wrote to all midwives stressing the need to call on medical aid for all cases of premature birth (as recommended by the CMB) and pointing out that attendance on Sundays was just as necessary as on other days of the week. There may have been a reluctance to call for medical help for which fees had to be paid, but the 1918 Maternity and Child Welfare Act stated that in cases of complicated midwifery, the fees of doctors called in by midwives for an 'emergency' in connection with a confinement must be paid, if necessary, in whole or in part by the local authority. Yet even with all this support and education, the cost of engaging a midwife must have been prohibitive. Dr Gibson's 1920 report reveals over forty per cent of Wakefield's confinements took place in the mothers' homes without a midwife in attendance. The training period for midwives was extended again in 1926 – making it a year before a woman could sit her CMB exam (six months for a trained nurse).

As well as the midwives who practised on a 'self-employed' basis, and those at the hospital, Wakefield Corporation commenced a district midwife service in 1927, employing just one woman to the role. A further appointment was made in 1930. Earnings for midwives were from 25s to £2 per case, so the Wakefield midwife who attended an exceptional 285 cases in one year must have earned at least £350, although undoubtedly she would have had expenses to pay from this sum. Midwives working under District Nursing Associations were salaried at £120 to £200 a year, less costs for accommodation. By the mid-1930s, all Wakefield's midwives were trained and CMB certified.

Increased demand for home nursing, including maternity cases, led to more staff being employed by the Wakefield Victoria District Nursing Association. This association had been in place since the nineteenth century, when it was proposed the council fund a home for two nurses and add another nurse to the team, to commemorate Queen Victoria's Diamond Jubilee in 1897. Demand for its services had grown steadily, then rapidly, until in 1935, the 21,785 visits made to 930 cases were double those of five years earlier.

Clearly the seven nurses and one superintendent now in place were over-worked and more district nurses were required. But where to accommodate them? An appeal was launched in 1936, to raise £6,000 for a new nurses' home as a memorial to the late King George V. By April 1938, the new home at 10, South Parade was ready to accommodate fourteen nurses, although only £3,000 had been raised. A further appeal was made for donations and another £2,000 was pledged by the year end.

One midwife who joined the Wakefield District Nursing team was Ida Lessons, who'd trained in Mansfield after the elderly uncle she was nursing passed away. Undeterred by her experience as a probationer, where she'd assisted in an arm amputation, she worked in various towns and cities, gaining experience. She qualified as a midwife in 1935 and worked in Leeds until 1940, when the opportunity to move to Wakefield was presented. The council allocated her a three-bedroom house – 28, Spa Grove – on the Lupset estate. It meant she could accommodate her bedridden mother, Martha, in the downstairs parlour and there was also room for her sister, Willow (whose husband was serving in the war) and baby nephew. This predominantly female household supported its hardworking breadwinner (Ida delivered nearly all the babies in Lupset during the war, and over 2,500 during her career), with Willow doing the household tasks and Martha acting as a useful secretary by answering the phone placed beside her bed. Ida was often found cycling the streets of Lupset in the blackout during the small hours of the morning. As well as delivering babies, she trained a series of pupil nurses who lodged at Spa Grove with them, including several well-qualified Jewish refugees whose non-British qualifications were not recognised.

The various phases of maternity and child welfare work, which evolved into a comprehensive organisation, were based on education, prevention and the provision of midwives and facilities. Even before the National Health Service was founded, infant mortality had fallen by around seventy-five per cent and infant sickness was so reduced that the scourge of potentially fatal summer diarrhoea virtually disappeared in Wakefield. Children's physique had improved and there were few cases of rickets.

One of the key benefits of the work though was psychological. The friendly relationships fostered between the female health visitors and the women under their charge helped to relieve the anxieties brought by often difficult duties of motherhood, by empowering mothers with knowledge and a sense of responsibility.

The Babies Welcome continued its work alongside the NHS until June 1956, when a decision was made to wind up the organisation. With mothers and babies now being better cared for by the state, it was felt the need for which it was founded, fifty years earlier, had disappeared.

Keeping a good home

Even with better maternity and infant care provision, fulfilling the traditional role as a homemaker, providing a welcoming, comfortable and healthy environment for their families, was a huge struggle for many Wakefield women. Dr Gibson's 1907 report described the various housing conditions in Wakefield. Although there were excellent residential parts in the town and working-class dwellings built since the adoption of building byelaws were also generally very good, there remained a considerable proportion of housing built before 1877, which had been constructed back-to-back or without through ventilation. Many of these old homes were situated in numerous cramped yards approached by narrow passages off the main thoroughfares of Kirkgate, Northgate and Westgate. These insanitary houses had been condemned on numerous occasions but had been patched up and re-let by private landlords.

Yards had been a feature of Wakefield's architecture since the nineteenth century and the number grew from thirty-four in 1847, to over 150 in the early-twentieth century. Even in 1850, this type of accommodation was giving cause for concern as outbreaks of smallpox and cholera took hold.

An 1851 enquiry into conditions estimated there were around 13,000 people (more than a quarter of the population) living in yards that were in the filthiest state, where there was little, if any, drainage. Water supply was inadequate and impure, with only around 200 'service-cocks' for the 2,700 houses. A table drawn up by William R. Milner, resident surgeon at the House of Correction, shows within these yards were 370 open cesspools, 241 pigsties, 174 stable and cowhouses and 516 privies. All contributed to the stench and damp, which oozed into the fabric of the buildings. Some houses accommodated as many as fourteen people, particularly when they squeezed in lodgers to help pay the rent.

The situation did not improve much either. In 1869, a further report by Dr John Netten Radcliffe, an expert in epidemiology, described conditions in several of Wakefield's yards. Hartley's, one of the many off Kirkgate, was 12ft wide, narrowing to 10ft. It had eight cottages, with windows only into the yard, where the surface-only drainage was clogged with slops and other liquid refuse, which spread out into filthy puddles. Within the yard lay sundry pigsties, a large middenstead at the level of the yard with attached privy, a foul-smelling enclosure and outhouse joined to the slaughterhouse of a pork butcher. There was a lair and cartshed, another midden with four privies – one open and 'inexpressibly foul'. A water stand-pipe was fixed near the slaughterhouse, and there was another pump. Liquid refuse from the slaughterhouse formed offensive pools as it flowed through the yard towards a drain hole. Eight households, with thirteen children under 10 years old, occupied Hartley's Yard, including Joseph Horn, the butcher, with his wife and five daughters.

Day's Yard off the east of Kirkgate wasn't much better. It was home to thirty-three people who lived in decrepit cottages around a yard barely 6ft wide, littered with rubbish. Its privy (just one) and middenstead were in a foul state and the surface drain was choked, causing a pool of stinking liquid to form. The local authority had also allowed an 8ft-high wall to be built 3ft from the doors of the two end cottages, so not only was there little ventilation, there was not much light either.[27]

That such poor housing continued to exist into the twentieth century seems incredible. Even in the late 1910s, insanitary conditions continued to cause real issues for the inhabitants. Tuberculosis mortality was 2½ times the city's average; infant mortality seventy-five per cent higher.

Time and again Dr Gibson reported that numbers of houses needed to be closed. He knew the solution lay in provision of cheap habitable homes by the council and the gradual demolition of slum property, yet the council did little. In one instance they closed only fourteen of the eighty-eight condemned by Gibson, and then, after repairs had been carried out, allowed them to be reopened.

One success he did have was ensuring houses were at least supplied with clean, mains water, with the final two houses in the city being connected in 1920. Toilets were a different matter. In 1909 there were 1,664 ash privies and 1,034 tub closets in Wakefield, which were slowly converted into flushing toilets at the rate of about 100 per year. Even in 1935, there remained forty-seven houses without a proper toilet.

Wakefield's population grew by around twenty-two per cent between 1901 and 1930, and with the corporation extending its responsibilities for a further 8,500 people when it included Sandal (in 1909) and Lupset (in 1921) within its boundaries, housing resources were stretched. Demolishing homes meant people needed rehousing, but private enterprise did nothing to provide for those who could only afford low rents. Just 1,270 houses were built in the fourteen years between 1900 and 1913, hardly sufficient to house the growing population, let alone provide new accommodation for those whose houses were unfit for habitation. In January 1913, a small committee consulted with Dr Gibson and agreed to tackle the worst slums in the Westgate area. Plans were to be prepared to build an initial thirty houses to be let at 3s 6d a week. Moving forward slowly, sites were identified in 1914, but everything stalled due to the outbreak of war. Even private house-building ground to a halt and there were only a further 150 or so new houses built in Wakefield between 1913 and 1920. The war also meant the action to close many insanitary areas was postponed and the houses remained inhabited. By 1918, the marked deterioration in housing conditions was obvious.

With the passing of the Housing and Town Planning Act 1918, reminding local authorities of their duties, extensive housing inspection was carried out in Wakefield. Around 1,175 houses were condemned, but these didn't include all the back-to-backs, thought to be about 3,400 in number. The Housing Act was ambitious, promising government subsidies to councils to develop new housing and rented accommodation for working people – to build homes fit for the heroes returning from the war.

The council agreed that around 2,000 new homes were needed and the four schemes in hand were announced in the

Yorkshire Post and Leeds Intelligencer, on 31 December 1919. The first site, at Elm Tree Street, would provide sixty-four two- and three-bedroom homes, due for occupation in the early spring of 1920, and a further forty-six were to be started at Rufford Street, Alverthorpe. The recently secured site at Portobello would provide nearly 500 new homes, and there were plans in place to build 900 houses on the newly-acquired Thornes House estate, although this scheme was later rejected.

Initial rents for a two-bedroom house with a scullery and living room were 8*s* a week, with water rates (for the hot and cold running water and indoor bathrooms) payable on top. A three-bedroom property was 10*s* a week, with a further 2*s* 6*d* if the house had a parlour. This was far higher than the 3*s* 6*d* proposed in 1913, but below the economic expectations of £32 10*s* annually. At this time a coalminer was paid around 20*s* a week and a well-paid skilled worker around 80*s*.

Clearance schemes continued with a blitz on old property in the Kirkgate area early in 1923, when a new road was made into Warrengate. The property owners of the 'wretched insanitary alleys or yards' were unhappy at the values paid for the compulsory purchases, but were assured they would receive market value. It was hoped the dispossessed tenants would willingly move to the new housing 'colony' at Portobello, close to the old Castle Hill at Sandal. Another new estate, the largest, was commenced at Lupset in 1924, where almost 2,000 houses were built, twenty per cent with a parlour.

By 1930, Wakefield had around 2,700 council houses and the Eastmoor and Darnley estates were already in the planning when further clearances were directed by the 1930 Housing Act. Assisted by subsidies for rehousing, Wakefield implemented another programme in 1933, to build the Peacock Farm and Flanshaw estates. In July 1937, the *Yorkshire Post and Leeds Intelligencer* reported the 4,000th house had been built by the Wakefield Corporation. The programme, once complete, meant around 4,900 new homes had been built at a cost to the council of over £2.25 million, including creating the infrastructure of roads, lighting and drainage.

As with most municipal housing schemes, the developments were situated at the boundaries of the urban sprawl, adjoining pleasant countryside. Estates were well laid out and incorporated open spaces. Houses had front and back gardens (usually generous, with space to grow fruit and vegetables) and roads were wide and tree-lined. As Dr Gibson commented as he retired in 1935, 'the estates are a delight to the eye and a credit to the city'.[28]

What the women of Wakefield felt about the upheaval from the communities they'd lived in I can only conjecture from anecdotal sources from my own family, which reveal most women were in raptures over the size and number of rooms, the 'mod cons' and the garden space of their new homes. A far cry from the cramped and insanitary conditions they'd endured for decades. The extraordinary progress made in municipal housing provided for population growth, relieved overcrowding and enabled clearance work to be implemented, and was a great contribution to the well-being of the wives and mothers of the city, whose role it was to keep their families safe, comfortable and healthy.

CHAPTER SIX

Wakefield's Active Citizens

Despite having no vote, women did have a voice and were always involved as active citizens in Wakefield, although in earlier times it was generally only women with some financial support from men who could make themselves heard a little. Most influence was through supporting causes either by subscription, fundraising or volunteering their time with groups of like-minded women.

One early example is the women subscribing to the upkeep of Wakefield's House of Recovery in the early 1850s, who outnumbered men six to one. However, the list mainly includes wives, widows and sisters of the prominent men of Wakefield and is similar to those included as nobility in *Slater's Directory* of 1855. Were these women simply carrying on the good work of their late husbands, or were they, as widows with money at their disposal, freer to support the causes they cared about? It is impossible to tell, but as educated women it is likely they were frustrated by their lack of influence.

Even as early as the 1860s, Wakefield's women were campaigning for suffrage. It was reported in various newspapers on 7 June 1866, that a 'curious petition' had been presented to Parliament by John Stuart Mill, MP for the City of Westminster. Influenced by his wife Harriet's views on women's rights, Mill had been elected in 1865 on a manifesto that included votes for women.

The petition, praying for the extension of suffrage to female householders, was signed by 1,550 ladies. It stated all who signed belonged to the upper and middle classes and were householders. Each gave their address, with six of the signatories from Wakefield.

Ada Marianne Barmby was the second wife of Rev. John Goodwyn Barmby (former Chartist, feminist and utopian socialist) of Wakefield Unitarian Chapel,[29] the daughter of Edward Shepherd, governor of Wakefield House of Correction. Miss Julia Maria Barmby was Goodwyn's sister, who, in 1872, had help found, and was secretary of, the Wakefield branch of the National Society for Woman's Suffrage, after Madam Ronniger's lecture on 'Female Suffrage' to a small but attentive audience in Wakefield in the February. Miss Mary Scholes Roach of Westgate was a schoolmistress (the aforementioned 'Ladies' School Luminary'), but doesn't appear to have been a householder, and another schoolmistress, Miss Annie O'Dwyer ran a boarding and day school in Northgate. Mrs Marianne Briggs of Outwood Hall, was the wife of Henry Briggs, a coal proprietor, and Clara Maria Clarkson of Hatfeild Road, born at Alverthorpe Hall in 1811, the daughter of solicitor Benjamin Clarkson (and cousin of Henry Clarkson, author of *Memories of Merrie Wakefield*). The sixth Wakefield signatory was listed as A. Norridge of Northgate, but is likely to be Mrs Ann Horridge of Northgate, wife of George Horridge, a well-known bookseller and printer.

The branch was still campaigning in the 1880s as recorded by a meeting at the Corn Exchange on 17 April 1882, where Alice Scatcherd, Mrs Shearer, Miss Carbutt, Mrs McCormick, Mrs Ellis, Mrs Vero (of Batley) and the Rev. John Wolstenholme and Rev A. B. Matthews all spoke for the cause. However, the society appears to have lost its momentum after the Barmbys moved back to their East Anglian roots and it lapsed until the 1900s.

In the meantime, the women of Wakefield continued to work hard to improve the lives of their sisters.

Looking after wayward girls

After the Wakefield Refuge and Reformation School became the West Riding Industrial Home for Discharged Female Prisoners in 1866, losing its government grant, the institution relied solely on voluntary efforts to continue its rehabilitation of female offenders. Although a subscription list had always been in operation, additional financial contributions now became absolutely necessary, and public appeals were issued. It also required new direction. The West Riding magistrates, seeing a potential candidate, asked Charlotte Emily Armytage, wife of Captain Godfrey Armytage, the new governor of Wakefield gaol, if she would become honorary superintendent and reorganise the women's work. She agreed and was appointed on 15 February 1866. Her unpaid role was to act as a medium of communication between the committee and the paid servants of the home. It involved frequent visits to the home, inspecting the matron's journal weekly and reporting to the committee quarterly on the general conduct of the inmates and the condition of the home. She also produced an annual report. With regard to the inmates, she was to inquire into any applications made for those who were ready for discharge, plus she had authority to expel any inmate who was unsuitable for the home's care.

At the outset, Mrs Armytage was assisted by Miss Marion Pitcher, head matron, and Miss Charlotte Elizabeth Spurgin, assistant matron, who both worked at the home for seven years, and widow Elizabeth Dean, laundress. They were obliged to live in the home and matron's role was a wide-reaching managerial position, with responsibility for all provisions, clothing, furniture and bedding. Matron's journal and accounts were to be open to inspection by the honorary supervisor at all times and she was to strictly observe the rules and orders of Mrs Armytage and the committee.

St John's provided accommodation for girls aged from early-teens to early-20s, although (as observed in the 1871 census) girls as young as 10 could be admitted. In 1867, the home hit a financial crisis and almost had to close, until Colonel Ackroyd guaranteed and paid the £70 annual rent and deposited a £200 fund in the bank. The home also made its own efforts to raise capital:

> Industrial Home for Discharged Female Prisoners. This institution, which is intended to afford a home for females when discharged from prison, is in need of help; and yesterday a sale of fancy and other goods was commenced in the Church Institution, at Wakefield, in aid of its funds. The institution has been in existence some time, but after the girls sentenced to be kept in a Reformatory were removed to the Reformatory at Doncaster, there were some fears that it might have to be given up. By the exertions of Mrs Godfrey Armytage (wife of Captain Armytage, governor at the West Riding Prison) there is no longer fear of such a result, though at the same time increased help in subscriptions is greatly required, There are now twenty-five or twenty-six women in the institution, and they are trained for industrial employment as domestic servants; and, when fitted, there is no difficulty experienced in obtaining situations for them. The income of the institution from donations and subscriptions is about £200 a year; and, by the work of the inmates in plain sewing and washing, this is increased to about £400. More, however, is wanted; and if the income could be increased, so could the number of inmates. We believe that Mrs Godfrey Armytage would gladly receive subscriptions, as would also Mr C. H. Binstead, of Wakefield, the secretary. At the sale of goods yesterday, the stalls were well-stocked, and were presided over by ladies of the town and neighbourhood.

Leeds Mercury, 24 April 1868

New subscribers and helpers came forward and a further £342 (including the proceeds of the sale) was added to the fund. With the work continuing successfully, more spacious accommodation was sought and in late October 1870, several West Riding towns contributed stalls at a week-long fund-raising bazaar held at Wakefield Corn Exchange. The sum realised (with other generous support) was in excess of £5,000 and this allowed the purchase of a larger, neighbouring property at St John's, which was duly converted and furnished and officially opened on 3 April 1872.

The *Leeds Mercury* described the 'most elegant and commodious building, which owes its origin in great part to the noble self-denying efforts of Mrs Godfrey Armytage' as occupying a commanding position and 'calculated in every way to answer the purposes of a comfortable house of reformation and training in habits of thrift and industry of girls discharged from prison'. As well as a ground floor appropriated to laundry work, with offices above, there was a second floor, which, alongside the dormitories, had a beautiful little chapel, extensively decorated by donations from friends of the institution.

New staff joined Charlotte Armytage's team, Miss Mary Jane Williams as matron, Mary A. Cooper and Julia Jane Jackman as assistant matrons, Emma Madison and Annie Adams to assist Elizabeth Dean in the laundry, plus Maria Bolton, cook, Mary Lambert, domestic servant, and a teacher, Alice Dean (probably Elizabeth Dean's daughter). Few of the thirty or so residents were from Wakefield, and it was noted that life in the home was 'at least a preventative against evils elsewhere and at a very critical period in their lives' and that 'a fence at the top of the cliff is better than a rescue at the bottom'. Julia Jackman was promoted to matron and was still in the post in 1911, thirty-nine years later.

By 1894, the home was bringing in money for its upkeep, with earnings from laundry work at around £850. At the home's AGM it was recorded that thirty-seven women had been admitted in the previous twelve months, twenty-three from prisons and the remainder either to be saved from conviction or because they were unmanageable in their own homes. Fifteen women had been sent into service, six restored to friends, four removed by friends, two sent to the workhouse, two expelled, one sent to a laundry for further training, another to Horbury House of Mercy and two had absconded – the first cases in nine years.[30]

It was also receiving great support from a team of lady visitors, women whose voluntary work included reading to and instructing the inmates and assisting in carrying out the objectives of the home. They were authorised to bring notice of any irregularities or matters worthy of attention, to the honorary inspector.

These visitors included Lady Catherine Milnes Gaskell of Thornes House, Mrs Eden, the bishop's wife, the vicar's wife, Mrs Donne, the Misses Caroline and Margaret Blomefield of 4, St John's North, the Misses Mary Isabel and Frances Margaret Smithson of 22, St John's Square, Miss Edith Wright of 91, Northgate, Miss Lucy Stanway Micklethwaite of 8, Bond St and Miss Edith Grace Mackie of 2, St John's Square. They were also subscribers to the home and generously held picnics and parties in their own homes for the girls.

By 1903, some thirty-seven years since its inception, the home had helped a total of 1,112 women. Of the £1,246 9s 9d income that year, £875 was from laundry and sewing. Matrons' salaries costs were around £210 and food was £305. Beneficial weekly classes were conducted by Miss Edith Mackie on Sunday afternoons, on Fridays by Miss Blomefield and during the week by Miss Raynor. Miss Scott had paid for a course of cookery lessons from a certificated teacher and there were other gifts and donations from various good women of the city and even former inmates.

All clothing for use of the inmates while in the house and their outfits on leaving was prepared in the work room. Bread was also kneaded and baked in the kitchen and the girls were taught housework. In addition to laundry work, sewing, and knitting their own stockings, those who showed any aptitude were taught how to cook. It meant the home could send girls into service as laundry maids or general servants, with the majority doing exceptionally well and earning good wages.[31]

Considering the poor starts in life experienced by many of these girls, it was a great achievement.

Of course there were a few exceptions. Constance Lee, described by the *York Herald* newspaper as a 'good-looking, neatly-dressed young woman of 19', had been an inmate of the home since 1892, after serving a month's sentence for theft in York in the January. But on 22 January 1893, she returned to a life of crime, stealing two petticoats, a pair of stockings, a pair of stays, a bodice, chemise, vest, handkerchief, pair of boots and 14s 6d from the home. She also stole a skirt, jacket, purse and £2 10s from Miss Mabel Marsh, the housekeeper. In April she was sentenced to three months' imprisonment with hard labour, but it appears she did not reform. By August she was out of prison and back in court, this time for stealing a gold brooch, cufflinks and rings in York. She was committed to prison once more, for six months with hard labour. As someone who had been in the home and reconvicted, she was not allowed back.

Emily Parker from Guildford had worked in various jobs before being sent to a similar home in Peckham, presumably by her parents. She was transferred to the Wakefield home in November 1898, aged 15. On 12 January 1900, she left the home for a position at Campsall Hall, Doncaster, home of Frederick Bacon Frank, a West Riding magistrate. While there she 'fell' and returned to St John's, apparently ill, but obviously pregnant.[32] She was hastily married in Market Weighton, on 30 March 1903, to Frederick Barker, an apprentice blacksmith from Campsall. At least Emily found marriage and motherhood. She and her husband went to live in Guildford with her father and had more children. But she wasn't the only girl to be labelled 'fallen'. Many suffered a similar fate and were stigmatised by 'losing (or being robbed of) their virtue', while the men, it seems, got on with their lives.

On 15 May 1919, Charlotte Emily Armytage passed away aged 88. She had no children and the home had been her life's work. For fifty-five years as honorary superintendent, she'd appointed the matrons, learned about the girls and their circumstances and kept in touch with a great many of them after they had left. New management was needed, and the strong character and high values of Charlotte would be difficult to replicate. Fortunately, Miss Edith Grace Mackie, a long-term supporter of the home and other good causes, stepped into the breach. At 66 years of age, many women might have been thinking about retirement, but not Edith, whose other work with the Wakefield District Nursing Association continued into the 1930s. Edith appointed Miss Trevers as head matron and the numbers increased to fifty. She made many changes to the girls' lives, work and dress and introduced new skills, such as knitting and embroidery. By 1921, with increasing costs of materials and food, plus work needing to be done on the fabric of the building, the committee found itself in financial difficulties. The trustees approached the Wakefield Diocesan Council with a view to taking over the institution and its preventative and rescue work for girls and young women, and on 1 January 1922 the diocese took possession of the home.

By this time the home was used for preventative work rather than rescue, and prided itself on the training for domestic service of:

1. Girls in dangerous surroundings from their home or from domestic service, sent by preventative workers in other towns or dioceses.

2. Girls of good character and average mental development sent by Guardians.

They were not to be regarded as bad girls, but some were difficult and required special care in their treatment and training. The new management thought this might be better achieved with smaller numbers and aimed for a limit of thirty-five. Teachers of various subjects were provided through Wakefield Education Authority and a Girl Guide company was founded.

In 1937, the home became an approved school for senior girls under the Children and Young Persons Act of 1933, but remained under the control of the diocese. It was known as St John's Home Training School. Its work in training girls for service continued, as adverts for a laundry matron in 1938 and sewing matron in 1939 'who must be accustomed to training difficult girls' demonstrate. The St John's Community Home, as it became known in the 1970s, continued to look after difficult girls until its closure in the 1980s.

The Mothers' Union

Another diocesan organisation with the lives of young women at heart was the Mothers' Union. The first meeting of the Wakefield Diocesan Mothers' Union was held on 7 October 1895 at Woodsome Hall, Huddersfield, the Yorkshire residence of Augusta, Dowager Countess of Dartmouth. The council passed three resolutions:

1. Members must be married women.
2. Associates to be members of the Church of England.
3. Unmarried women could join as associates.

It joined the confederation of existing Mother's Union (MU) organisations and adopted the MU constitution, promoting three central objects:

1. To uphold the sanctity of marriage.
2. To awaken in mothers of all classes a sense of their great responsibility as mothers in the training of their boys and girls as the future fathers and mothers of England.
3. To organise in every place a band of mothers who will unite in prayer and seek by their own example to lead their families in purity and holiness of life.

Each member was asked to carry out the principles of the MU in her own home in the best way she could, and to depend more upon individual work than upon meetings.

By the end of the first year, the president (Augusta Dartmouth) was able to report the diocese had eight branches and almost 200 members and their work was steadily extending from one parish to another. One of the concerns in growing the membership was the notion that the MU was for poor mothers only. The attitude of some highly educated mothers towards the organisation was one of kindly and condescending patronage. Snobbery abounded – 'the poor mothers do so need to be told of their duties, they neglect them sadly', and 'the Mothers' Union is so good for the lower classes', etc.

The president circulated a letter from the MU's founder, Mary Sumner (whose original plan was to call on women of all social classes to support one another and to see motherhood as an important profession), in which she articulated that many poor mothers were infinitely superior in their self-sacrifice, patient endurance and simple obedience to duty, and there was a lot to learn from them. The president also suggested their union might be of use in raising a higher sense of the responsibilities of fathers in the upbringing of children and encouraged branches to arrange meetings and services to occasionally include men.[33]

After the death of Augusta Dartmouth in December 1900, Mrs Anna Louisa Milnes-Gaskell of Lupset Hall, Wakefield became president, taking office in September 1901. She remained president until January 1915, when the impact of the First World War was beginning to be realised. Over the fourteen years the diocesan branch had grown from thirty branches and around 1,000 members to 148 branches with a membership of 8,600 and her resignation was to allow the good work to be continued by a younger, more energetic woman (Anna was almost 70). The baton was passed to Mrs Beatrice Lister-Kaye of Denby Grange, a mere youngster of 53.

In her report, Anna related how when she'd joined the Mothers' Union in 1897, life had seemed very empty (Gerald had passed away that year) but the work and support from other women had made her happy and fulfilled. She had friendships that would last into eternity and would continue as a member. Referring to the supreme crisis in their lives, where men were enlisting for war, leaving the non-combatant women at home, she spoke of the MU's opportunity to enrol women, especially those in need of sympathy and prayer. She advised wisely how a personal touch of interest could do much to prevent the thoughtless spending of money, lack of interest in their homes and neglect of their children, by those who were lonely and exposed to 'special temptations'.[34]

In addition to spiritual help, the MU engaged itself in practical activities. Weekly collections were undertaken to help welcome the Belgian refugees being given shelter in Wakefield, friendly preparations made and tender attention shown to their children. The ladies knitted socks and balaclavas and provided chocolate, plum puddings and tobacco for Christmas stockings for not only British wounded soldiers and men at the front but also the French wounded and interned Belgian soldiers. One member, an invalid, rallied her friends and collected £5 worth of pipes to be sent to France.

And instead of an exciting journey by train, the branch's annual festival in 1915, was a stay-at-home affair – a rightful economy prescribed by time of war. Nonetheless, a well-attended service in the cathedral was followed by a plentiful tea. A bookstall sold 300 penny cookery books, and in the evening the mothers wandered or sat in a restful and spacious garden, thrown open by one of the members, until darkness fell. It must have been a welcome respite from the worries and troubles of the time.

Socialist women campaigners

Another active women's group, the Women's Co-operative Guild, was inaugurated in Wakefield around the same time as the Mothers' Union, but with a very different approach to improving the lives of women.

The Women's League for the Spread of Co-operation had been established in 1883, by Lady Alice Sophia Acland, who edited the 'Women's Corner' of the *Co-operative News*, and Mary Lawrenson, a teacher who suggested the creation of an organisation to promote instructional and recreational classes for mothers and girls. It changed its name to the Women's Co-operative Guild in

1884, and within five years there were fifty-one branches. Their purpose was to give women a voice within the co-operative movement, where only men seemed to attend meetings, with a key aim of training women co-operative society members to take responsible positions within the movement, stressing the power to be derived from membership. It was said being a member of the Guild 'built confidence, opened doors into all areas of public life, and made its members feel special'.

Wakefield's branch was set up in 1898, but only the minute books commencing April 1908 are available. These first minutes report that the women's suffrage papers were read and a letter had been received from the local MP's secretary regarding votes for women. As club secretary, Miss Boileau was nominated to attend the Guild's twenty-fifth annual congress at Burton-on-Trent on 23 June, but found it would be impossible to do so. Two other nominees, Mrs March and Mrs Bedford also declined and it is not clear whether anyone from Wakefield did eventually make the journey. The congress discussed women's suffrage and the committee presented a resolution calling on the government to include women's enfranchisement in the next electoral reform Bill. Other issues discussed were the education of girls, old age pensions and the eligibility of married women for town and county councils.

With Miss Boileau resigning from her secretarial role in June, citing ill-health, a new committee, consisting of Mrs Sarah Shepley, president, Mrs S.H. Crowe, vice-president, Mrs Oxley, secretary, Mrs Bedford, assistant secretary and Mrs Jacques as club secretary, was elected in August 1908. One of their first tasks seems to have been to organise a children's tea for early January 1909, for which 300 tickets had been sold. The provisions list included six sandwich loaves, 16lbs meat to be made into potted meat, eight dozen teacakes (brown/white/currant), eight brown loaves at 3d each, 14lbs of slab cake, six dozen mixed sponge sandwich cakes, 200 scones (costing a total of 7s 2d), 12lbs of butter, 14lbs of sugar, 4lbs of tea and fifteen quarts of milk. It was obviously too generous a quantity, since it was later recommended by the secretary they should not order currant teacakes as well as scones. The following year's party was attended by twenty-two adults paying 6*d* a ticket and 180 children at 4*d* a ticket. Food costs had been £3 14*s* 2*d* and entertainment a further £1 8*s* 5*d*. Income from ticket sales, plus some sales of leftover food had totalled £3 19*s* 4*d*, so the Guild was slightly out of pocket by £1 3*s* 3*d*. Dissatisfaction was expressed about the cost of the entertainment, which included the hire of a lantern slide at 4*s* and the projectionist at 2*s* 6*d*.[35]

At the heart of the Guild's work was loyalty to the local society, the Co-operative Wholesale Society (CWS) and all co-operative production. This included buying the wide range of products manufactured by the CWS and encouraging others to do so. Members were mainly married women, and, as keen advocates of product quality and value for money, able to voice their opinions about the running of the society and its products.

One example of this is documented in the Wakefield Guild's meeting minutes of 9 October, 1909. Perhaps mindful of the winter nights drawing in, the ladies discussed the question of holding a 'cocoa night'.

Samples of cocoa had arrived from Luton CWS and each member was invited to try it at home. If the product was satisfactory they would hold a cocoa supper, promoting the Co-op product and raising funds by selling cocoa and biscuits to local women. The branch secretary, Mrs Hartley, promised to ask Mr Lyle – a representative from the cocoa works – if he could address the meeting, but if this was not possible, a member of the committee would read and distribute the pamphlets that had accompanied the samples.

However, their interests were far wider than just the family home and budget. In the same way as men were united by trade unions to address wages, Co-operative Women's Guild members were urged to use their collective powers to press for the national reforms needed in their lives as wives, housewives and mothers. They became increasingly politically active, campaigning for changes that would benefit women's lives, including equal pay, maternity benefits, public health and housing, representation on public bodies, women's suffrage and divorce law reform.

In 1909, when a Royal Commission was established to look into divorce laws, the Guild set up its own enquiry among members. As things stood at the time, a man could petition court to divorce his wife on the basis of adultery, which he had to prove. A woman, on the other hand, had to not only prove her husband had been unfaithful but also additional faults such as cruelty, incest or rape. Another barrier to divorce was the cost and the fact that proceedings were held in open courts, allowing personal details to be revealed.

The Guild was able to present its findings when the commission began to collect its evidence. At a sitting in Winchester House in London on 9 November 1910, Miss Margaret Llewellyn Davies, speaking on behalf of the members, informed the commission of the Guild's credentials. This self-governing organisation of women with connections to distributive industrial co-operative societies had 25,597 members in 520 branches – nearly all married women, whose husbands worked in ordinary trades. Their inquiry into divorce laws had revealed an overwhelming demand for drastic reform. She related that the guildswomen believed the present divorce laws were not only out-of-date compared with other Protestant European countries but also out of touch with the predominant opinion of the largest class of women. Divorce was a much-needed method of relief in cases where marriage ties involved a life of degradation and suffering for women and children. It was impossible to exaggerate the strength of feeling there should be equal moral standards for men and women and grounds for divorce should be the same. Although women could leave abusive marriages by obtaining separation orders on grounds of cruelty from their husbands, since these did not amount to divorce, they were unable to remarry. Miss Davies pointed out that cruelty needed to be interpreted as more than physical cruelty, and that an unfaithful husband was guilty of inflicting the most refined cruelty of all on his wife. On the question of divorce proceedings being cheapened, the feeling was very widespread that the poor should have the same chances as the rich. The issue of costs was of special importance to women, since most wives had no money of their own. They believed all costs, including the expenses of witnesses, must be state-paid where they could not be recovered from the husband and where the wife had no property (*Yorkshire Post and Leeds Intelligencer*, 10 November 1910).

The Women's Co-operative Guild was the only organised body of women to submit evidence to the commission and it afforded a stimulus for discussions, leading to successive resolutions calling for alterations to the law. Nothing changed and when divorce laws were raised again in the House of Commons in March 1914, the Guild issued a memorandum to members detailing its views.

These were discussed at the Wakefield branch meeting in October, but nothing is recorded as to whether there was agreement. Certainly the views were not well-received by the Co-operative movement. The *Yorkshire Post and Leeds Intelligencer*, 24 November 1914, reported a schism was threatened and the £400 grant to finance the Women's Guild was to be withdrawn:

> Some time ago the Guild gave expression to views, on the subject of divorce law reform, that were unpalatable to the controllers of the Co-operative Union, and after months of heated controversy it has now been decided that the subsidy to the Women's Guild is to be withdrawn until such time as the Guild finds convenient to develop less objectionable views on this subject. The women have taken offence at the terms of the ultimatum presented to them, and are determined to resist what they call male dictation in a matter of such importance to women. It is now a question of appealing to the whole membership to condemn or approve the stoppage of the subsidy. Meantime, the work of the Guild is considerably hampered by the stoppage of supplies.

When the Co-operative movement held its congress in May 1915, the matter was still not resolved. Mr G. Bastard presided over the question of the action of the Women's Guild over divorce law reform and the right of the board to withhold money from any organisation pursuing policy detrimental to the interests of the Co-operative movement. Claiming it had received contributions from Catholic co-operators and it was unfair to use money to finance a cause so objectionable to them, the grant would only be restored if the Guild ceased its agitation on divorce law reform. Mrs Pound, speaking on behalf of the women, moved that it was wrong for the board to stop the grant at the dictation of an outside sectarian body, and called for the congress to endorse the principle of self-government for the Women's Guild. However, at the vote the central board's resolution was carried and the grant continued to be withheld.

Although there were several attempts to push divorce reforms through Parliament it was not until August 1923 that the *Yorkshire Post* was able to announce that for the first time since 1918, a really triumphant note could be sounded by those interested in legislation affecting the interests of women and children. One of the three clauses entering the statute books was the short and simple Matrimonial Causes Act, which recognised equal moral standard in marriage and meant a wife could divorce her husband on the same grounds as a husband could divorce his wife – adultery. It was felt that better organisation among women citizens, plus a change in the spirit of the times and a sympathetic government had allowed progress to be made. Most of the suggestions of the Women's Guild had been ignored.

A further act in 1937, extended the grounds for divorce to include cruelty, desertion and incurable insanity, but even though more widespread, divorce was still uncommon and a potential source of shame for many women.

The campaign for women's suffrage

The women of Wakefield's campaign for women's suffrage began in earnest in 1910, when Miss Florence Beaumont, accompanied as always by her dachshund – named John Stuart Mill in honour of the great supporter of women's rights – hosted a drawing-room meeting at her Hatfeild Hall home on Thursday, 10 March. Forty-five ladies listened attentively to Miss Mary Fielden (Yorkshire organiser for the National Union of Women's Suffrage Societies (NUWSS)) speak about the various social and economic disabilities under which they laboured with their voteless condition, pointing out the various franchises qualifying men to vote applied equally to women. Twenty-six women heeded the call to join the NUWSS and it was hoped a Wakefield branch would soon be formed. Remaining in Wakefield for a few days, Mary Fielden spoke again at another drawing-room meeting on 19 March, this time the home of Mrs Eleanor Frances Atcherley (née Micklethwaite) at Haddon Leys, Sandal. Eleanor was the wife of the West Riding chief of police, Llewellyn William Atcherley, and because her work was an embarrassment to his position she later resigned from her role as chairman of the Wakefield branch. Another seven ladies joined the NUWSS and a public meeting was scheduled for 8 April at the Music Saloon. A provisional committee for the proposed affiliated branch was drawn up and by the first week in April the Wakefield branch had fifty members. Its meeting was well attended, and Liverpool preacher and suffragist Agnes Maude Royden made a stirring and convincing speech, explaining the policy and aims of the National Union. A further twenty-six women joined the branch. The members elected a president, Mrs Mary Amelia Livesey Lee (née Stonehouse) of St John's North, and secretary, Florence Beaumont, and a committee of nine members, on 28 April.[36]

Meetings continued throughout the summer, with various speakers invited and reports submitted to the *Common Cause* (a newspaper supporting NUWSS policies). Tuesday, 18 October was a red-letter day in the Wakefield Women's Suffrage Society history, when Millicent Garrett Fawcett joined the drawing-room meeting at Hatfeild Hall. She received a hearty welcome from a 'deeply interested audience' and her splendid speech filled the members with fresh courage and enthusiasm.

Debates, 'at homes', entertainment evenings, visits and speeches from prominent suffragists (including Isabella Ormston Ford and Mrs Edwin Gray) all helped to win new support and interest and by October 1911, the society had 156 members with an enlarged committee as follows:[37]

Chairman Committee	Mrs Eleanor Atcherley, Haddon Leys, Sandal.
Hon Treasurer	Mrs Alice Cleaver Hindmarsh, 27, Westfield Grove, Wakefield.
Hon Secretary	Miss Florence Beaumont, Hatfeild Hall, Wakefield.
Common Cause Secretary	Miss Maud Mary Spencer, 92, Lower York Street, Wakefield.
Assistant Clerical Secretaries	Miss Lilly Lee, Miss A. McArthur, Miss A.L. Preston.
Committee	Miss Carr, Mrs. Clarkson, Mrs T. Craven, Miss Eaton, Miss Alice Eaton, Miss Gill, Mrs Garrett, Miss Hick, Mrs Evelyn Maud Hirst of Acacia House, 1, Westfield Terrace, Mrs Annie Hudson of Grove Hall, Mrs Mary Amelia Livesey Lee, Mrs Reader, Miss Kate Spencer (sister of Maud), Mrs Southey (wife of Rev. G. Southey), Miss N. Walley, Mrs Agnes Florence Watmough of Hatfeild Villa, Hatfeild St, Mrs Sarah McLean Wilson of Snaizeholme, Blenheim Rd.

To raise new interest in suffrage work, the Wakefield society ran very successful '*Common Cause* Week' in the last week of October 1911. A team of women, led by Florence Beaumont, worked diligently to encourage a number of Wakefield businesses to place advertisements in the suffragist paper and local newsagents to stock it. Large strip posters were created for window advertising and the paper was also placed in the free library and one of the political clubs. As Wednesday, 1 November was municipal election day, women took the opportunity to sell the *Common Cause* outside polling stations. It was great propaganda, which gained further impetus when the Earl of Lytton (younger brother of Lady Constance Lytton, a leading suffragette) and Isabella Ford made eloquent and convincing speeches to an enthusiastic audience at a crowded public meeting at the Institute the same day. As a result of the women's endeavours twelve of Wakefield's newsagents agreed to stock and sell the *Common Cause*, raising continued awareness for the campaign. The week was hailed as a huge success and the work went on.

A sub-committee was appointed, tasked with dealing with Trade Union resolutions. Its secretary was Miss B.B. Rogers. In November 1912, the West Riding Federation organiser, Miss Allen, addressed the Wakefield Trades and Labour Council, which unanimously passed a resolution in support of women's suffrage. Isabella Ford explained the election fighting policy and urged the Wakefield WSS committee to lobby Labour organisations in the town. The women received huge support from the secretaries of the various Wakefield trade unions, who distributed literature, despatched postcards, sent copies of resolutions to leaders of parliamentary parties and passed resolutions of their own to support votes for women. It demonstrated to the MP that the Labour vote was pro-suffrage.

Excitement began to build as plans were drawn up in the spring of 1913 for a great pilgrimage, in which women would march peacefully from all corners of England and Wales to Hyde Park, London, arriving on 26 July. Ladies' outfitters, Swan and Edgar of Regent Street and Piccadilly, advertised their special attire for the pilgrimage. As well as manila straw hats trimmed with ribbon in the National Union colours of green, white and red, the 'serviceable attire at moderate prices' included the 'Boyden' tailor-cut walking skirt – a button-through full-length skirt available in black, navy or cream coating, Irish linen, piqué or drill, and the 'Dumfries' – a tailored coat and skirt for seaside and country wear, made of all-wool shrunk flannel.[38] These cannot have been comfortable nor light garments for such a long walk in mid-summer, and it is a testament to the strength of the movement that many women walked the whole way.

The Wakefield women joined the Great North Road pilgrims, who had started in Newcastle on 17 June, and arrived, as scheduled, in Wakefield on 2 July. All did not go well.

On 11 July, *The Common Cause* reported:

> On Tuesday, we had a hot and dusty tramp to Wakefield, [from Leeds] relieved by a rest in a hayfield, and another in Mrs. Macarthur's [sic] shady orchard. At Outwood tea was provided by the Wakefield Society, a large meeting was held, and in the evening we marched into the town [led by Florence Beaumont carrying the branch banner]. Here an immense crowd was awaiting us. We had three platforms [two in Calder Vale Road and one at the junction of Ings Road and Kirkgate] and the speakers, Mrs. [Helena] Renton, Mrs. Oldham, Miss [Ida] Beaver, Miss Hannah Burgess, and others, exchanged platforms at intervals. The resolution was carried at each meeting, but after the demonstration was ended the Pilgrims had some unpleasant experiences, mainly owing to the inadequate police arrangements. In spite of the warnings given them by the Wakefield Society, the local police were totally unprepared for so large a meeting, and neglected to provide for the safe passage of the speakers at its close. The hooligan element on the outskirts of the crowd, unable to hear the speeches, had grown restless, and, fearful lest so unique an occasion should pass without excitement, proceeded to hustle the Pilgrims. A stone was thrown at one of the speakers, giving her a black eye, and in the general scrimmage most of us were more or less bruised. One Pilgrim had to return home the next day with a slightly injured spine, and another had her foot badly hurt. The police at last came to the rescue, shelter was given in a neighbouring garage, and we eventually got away in taxis. As at Ripon, it was found that the Pilgrims had been preceded in Wakefield by the

Anti-Suffragists. I have witnesses who can vouch for my statement that at the Anti-Suffrage meeting held in Wakefield on Tuesday night, one of the speakers incited his audience to break up our meeting the next evening. A special service was held at St. Michael's Church on Wednesday morning before the Pilgrims left Wakefield. The Vicar, Mr J. G. Love, conducted the service, and Canon Welch, the Vicar of Wakefield, gave an excellent address. At Barnsley, Rotherham, and Sheffield we have had magnificent demonstrations, and meetings have been held wherever sufficient crowds were gathered all along the route. An amusing incident occurred at the evening meeting at Barnsley, when a drunken interrupter of vast proportions was invited to voice his opinions from one of the platforms. Said a diminutive but very resolute Yorkshire woman to the crowd: 'Well, I'd nivver o' let yon ignorant article get on ont' platform I wish I wa' near. I'd have him darn.'

Although it is not recorded who the anti-suffragists were on the day, one person of note who was definitely anti-suffrage was Mrs Gwendoline Beaumont (née Haworth) who had married Florence's younger brother, Gerald, in June 1906. When Gerald was called up to the KOYLI in 1914, Gwendoline and her three young sons moved into Hatfeild House to live with Florence and her father and attend to the housekeeping. One wonders about the discussions that these capable and intelligent women might have had while living under the same roof. According to accounts by Stephen Beaumont, Gwendoline's eldest son, Gwendoline shared none of her sister-in-law's opinions on women's rights, believing that women did not need the vote since they could always make men do what they wanted by 'other means'. However, they got on excellently and did agree that the noisy activity of the militant suffragettes was counter-productive. Herbert Beaumont, Florence's father, was wholly tolerant of Florence's views and did not object to her work for female suffrage.

As war broke out, the Wakefield suffragists turned their attention to 'women's work in time of war'. Drawing-room meetings continued at members' homes, but campaigning and propaganda were replaced by fundraising. Dr Elsie Inglis, secretary of the Scottish Federation of the NUWSS, spearheaded a campaign to establish a Scottish Women's Hospital (SWH) for men wounded on active service, and an appeal was launched for all societies to assist. The aim was to equip and offer one hospital to the French Red Cross and one to the Serbian Red Cross, where there was urgent need of medical aid. Many women surgeons, nurses, medical students and VADs immediately volunteered to go abroad to staff the hospitals, so the appeal was for money and equipment, and as an incentive donors of £50 or £25 could name a bed for a year or six months. Bedding, bandages and hundreds of nightshirts and pairs of pyjamas were called for. By the end of November almost £5,000 had been raised and in December 1914, the *Common Cause* reported they 'were off at last'. A hospital party had arrived at Royaumont Abbey, nine miles from the nearest railway station at Chantilly, and was to set up the first hospital base there. In April 1915, Dr Inglis opened a second hospital in Serbia and this, combined with other support, meant the Scottish Women's Hospital was servicing 1,000 beds with 250 staff including nineteen female doctors.

The Wakefield WSS rallied to the cause, initially setting up a working party, which met at The Laurels, St John's, every Wednesday from 2.30 till 6.00 p.m. and again from 7.00 till 8.00 p.m. These sewing parties made up hospital garments, the materials being supplied ready to sew up. The meetings were well attended and it was soon recorded that a large parcel of bandages, swabs, clothing, and woollies had been despatched to the SWH offices in Edinburgh.[39]

At the annual meeting on 29 May 1916, it was reported that no propaganda work had been carried out in the previous twelve months, but the society continued to thrive. Fundraising in aid of the SWH had included a garden party at Field Head, and a whist drive. Over £76 had been collected, enabling the society to endow two 'Wakefield' beds in a third Serbian unit and buy more materials for the sewing parties. In addition, 193 dozen swabs, 446 bandages, and 319 hospital garments had been sent to the Edinburgh headquarters. Florence Beaumont had addressed the Women's Co-operative Guild and the Eastmoor and Sandal Patriotic Clubs on the work of the SWH. She also wrote an impassioned plea to the editor of the *Yorkshire Post* on 19 October 1916, asking the good folk of Wakefield to support the 'Lamp Day', which was to be held as a fundraiser on Saturday, 28 October. The 'day' was in memory of the 'Lady of the Lamp', Florence Nightingale, and the proceeds from sales of small coloured paper lamps were to be devoted to maintaining a 'Wakefield Bed' at the Royaumont hospital. Owing to the huge numbers wounded in the defence of Verdun and action on the Somme, it had been necessary to double the size of the hospital to 400 beds and support was urgently needed. Florence, hoping that no denizen of Wakefield would be without a lamp on the day, called for sellers and helpers to make the day a success.

While the sewing and fundraising work continued, when the question of a new parliamentary register was raised in 1916, it gave the NUWSS new impetus to assert that if voting rights were to be extended to more men, women should be given the vote too. With clear support from nearly all quarters, Prime Minister Herbert Asquith finally changed his view and agreed for the subject to be debated. Campaigning recommenced in earnest.

Wakefield once again welcomed Millicent Fawcett to a public meeting on 23 April 1917. Her inspiring address, in which she proposed a resolution welcoming the new bill and anticipating the speedy enfranchisement of women, was unanimously carried. The Bill for the Representation of the People Act was passed in the House of Commons on 19 June 1917 and after lengthy debates in the House of Lords finally received royal assent on 6 February 1918. It gave women over 30 who owned property (or whose husbands were property owners) the right to vote – approximately 8½ million women. It was a triumph of sorts.

Florence Beaumont's work was not only attached to the suffrage cause. She became honorary secretary of sub-committee of the Wakefield Women's Relief organisation and was once again to be found appealing to Wakefield readers of the *Yorkshire Post*, this time for food parcels for prisoners of war:

> To the Editor of the Yorkshire Post. Sir – may I appeal through your columns to those of your readers in Wakefield and district who are wishful to send weekly parcels of food to prisoners of war in Germany? The Mayoress of Wakefield (Mrs Stonehouse, West Parade) is chairman of a sub-committee which has been formed from a request from our Women's Relief Committee to deal with this matter and to prevent overlapping. Will anyone who wishes to help our men in Germany, who are so sorely in need of weekly parcels of food—which, I may mention, can be sent post free— communicate at once either with the Mayoress or with me? We hope to send each person the name of a prisoner of war to whom each week a parcel of such things as bread, tinned fruit, sardines, chocolate, tea, cigarettes, and so on can be sent. The KOYLI [Kings Own Yorkshire Light Infantry] and the West Yorkshires [Regiment] are now equipped with 'Fairy Godmothers', but we hope to get in touch with other regiments who are not so fortunate. We feel sure there are many women in Wakefield who will not forget the hardships that are being endured by our brave men in the prisoners' camps in Germany, and who will be glad each week to send a small parcel of food to show that they are not forgotten in their weary waiting for liberty.— Yours, etc., FLORENCE M. BEAUMONT. Joint Hon. Sec. Wakefield Women's Relief Sub-Committee. Hatfeild Hall, Wakefield, June 8, 1915.

With Gwendoline in charge of housekeeping, Hatfeild Hall was almost an open house during the war. When Herbert Beaumont answered an appeal for householders with spare rooms to take in Belgian refugees, the house became home to M. and Mme Petere and their son, 16-year-old Georges, who spoke no English. And as the casualty list from Gallipoli grew, a number of convalescing soldiers were given the very best care and compassion. Rising magnificently to the occasion, Gwendoline took all incursions in her stride and whatever her inner feelings and worries about the war, always kept a cheerful countenance.

Tireless volunteer

Another Wakefield woman who worked tirelessly to help servicemen during the war was Lady Catherine Milnes-Gaskell. In what seem like preparations for imminent war, she had been involved in a recruiting movement in Bradford in May 1912, which sought to increase the strength of not only the Territorial Army but the St John Ambulance brigade, so there would be a nucleus of trained men and women in all parts of the country, who could deal with the large number of sick and wounded who would certainly need attention if the country was engaged in a great war. Lady Catherine told the meeting they desired to fire the people of England, especially those in crowded towns, with a sense of their duty. They wanted a new spirit; the great spirit of self-sacrifice. Although women could not serve in the sense of being soldiers, they could serve in other ways and she believed the ambulance was a form of national service women could devote themselves to.

An ardent patriot, she spoke at a concert in aid of the city auxiliary fund held at Wakefield's Empire Theatre on 13 September 1914. Referring to the magnificent courage and devotion already exhibited by men of all classes during the greatest trial England had ever had, she asked the women of Wakefield 'not to grudge the giving of their dear ones, so England might maintain the great and high place she held among the civilised nations of the world'. The horror of what was to follow was soon apparent.

In her supervisory role as vice-president of two auxiliary hospitals (Clayton Hospital and Field House in Bradford), and ever mindful of the need of the wounded, she involved herself in practical work. Once the hospitals were up and running and receiving wounded men she made several appeals to *Yorkshire*

Post readers for donations to help the men recover. The letters poignantly illustrate the times they were living in:

> Appeal by Lady Catherine Milnes-Gaskell. To the Editor of the Yorkshire Post.
>
> Sir, We have at the Clayton Hospital accommodation for 48 men. The beds are now occupied by wounded soldiers. On last Friday we received our second batch, and these straight from the front. Some of them arrived very exhausted, but, thanks to the care of our devoted surgeon in charge, Mr T. Walker, and good nursing, our wounded men are now rapidly recovering. Mrs King, the Commandant of the VAD nurses, is most grateful for gifts of fruit, fresh eggs, game, rabbits, poultry, and jams, bacon, and hams. I am also starting a Shilling Fund, and should very grateful if any lady or gentleman would make an application to me for a collecting card, and use headed paper or business card, and so help our good work, as funds in a little while will be urgently needed. Anyone who is kind enough to send any gift is begged send it thus addressed: —The Commandant, Clayton VAD (Aux.) Hospital, Wakefield.—Yours, etc. CATHERINE MILNES-GASKELL. Thornes House. Wakefield, December 2, 1914.

On 16 August 1915, she appealed to the owners of grouse moors to send birds to the commandant and matron of the two military hospitals. Stating the wounded men were too ill to eat butcher's meat, therefore the grouse would fill a real want and give great pleasure to the men, added there was cold storage available to keep the supply fresh.

Whether the appeal was answered is not known, but certainly her call for apples in the autumn met with a good response, with the people of Wakefield donating very fine fruit, 2.6 tons of which had been sent to the brave Yorkshire troops at the front. A further consignment was due to be despatched immediately after Christmas.

Lady Catherine didn't merely distribute produce donated by others, she was willing to roll her sleeves up too as this, another letter to the *Yorkshire Post*, demonstrates:

BOTTLED FRUITS FOR THE WOUNDED.

Sir. — I should be most grateful if you would let it be known again that I am bottling all fruits obtainable for the wounded in my two districts, Wakefield and Bradford. I would be extremely grateful if any kind owners of gardens would send me in due course any gooseberries, carriage paid to this address, and I will bottle them for the benefit of the wounded soldiers. I should be grateful if they may be picked on the large size, and where possible tailed and nosed, but if this is impossible owing to difficulties of labour I will get them done here by the kindness of the Boy Scouts, who have helped me often in the past, and who have done such excellent work for our wounded both here and at Bradford – Yours, etc.. CATHERINE MILNES-GASKELL Thornes House, Wakefield, May 26, 1916.

After the death of her husband, the Right Honourable Charles Milnes-Gaskell, on 9 January 1919, at Thornes House, their home and estate was sold to Wakefield corporation and Lady Catherine retired to Much Wenlock in Shropshire. There she became a magistrate and also pursued her passion for gardening, providing facilities for women to learn gardening in the grounds of her Wenlock Abbey home. When she passed away on 21 August 1935, her obituary cited her wartime charitable and welfare work and also her fluency as a writer. In one of her books, *A Woman's Soul*, she presented the woman's aspect of war, illustrating her own experiences of the tragedy and suffering in the homes of the people of Wakefield.

Women in politics

As Florence Beaumont wrote in a piece on Women Citizens for the Wakefield Girls' High School Review in 1919, the war years had been significant in changing public opinion with regard to the position of women in the community. She knew there was still work to do, stating:

> There are attempts here and there to limit by statute the scope of women's activities, but on these we need not dwell. The walls of Jericho are down, and nothing in the future need limit or hinder the opportunities for useful work and service on the part of women, save their own indifference or failure to discern the signs of the times.[40]

Since the Local Government Act of 1894, women, irrespective of marital status, had had the right to elect, and also to stand for election on parish councils, district councils, school boards and Boards of Guardians as Poor Law administrators. Wakefield Union was no exception and had several women on its Board of Guardians. In 1929, however, with new legislation due to come into effect on 1 April 1930, handing over the functions of Boards of Guardians to county and county borough councils, there were fears that these important women would be lost to local politics. As things stood there were eighty-four County Borough Councils in England and Wales, with only 185 women serving and Wakefield was one of eleven district councils without any women.

Council elections scheduled for November 1929 provided an opportunity to elect women as local councillors, and the *Common Cause* especially urged women voters to 'Vote, Vote, Vote' to ensure the best candidates were elected. Five women candidates stood in the eleven Wakefield wards, two gaining seats on the council – Mrs Florence (known as Fanny) Wordsworth Stott (Conservative) for Eastmoor and Mrs Effie Hirst Crowe (Socialist) for North Westgate. Both had experience of committee work – Mrs Stott on Wakefield's Board of Guardians and Mrs Crowe as secretary of the Wakefield Socialist party and a co-opted member of Wakefield Education Committee (*Yorkshire Post and Leeds Intelligencer*, 26 November 1929).

Other women followed – Mrs Emily Constance Blakeley (née Fozzard) of 18 Buxton Place, Mrs Clara Abell (née Mellor) of 26 Peterson Rd, Mrs Margaret Louise Thomas (née Armstrong-Lamb) of Penrhyn, Westfield Grove and in 1950, Mrs Constance Hilda Blakeley (née Walton) of St John's Grove.[41] Apart from Clara Abell, who passed away in 1949, these were the only women serving on Wakefield's thirty-nine seat council in 1950. Interestingly the 1939 register lists them all as doing 'unpaid domestic duties', although Clara Abell and Mrs Clara Bonner Judge who wasn't on the council, but served on the Education Committee, were also noted as air-raid wardens.

Listing these women as doing 'unpaid domestic duties' does them a great disservice. As well as their council duties, all were involved in other social and voluntary roles. Emily Blakeley served alongside her husband on Wakefield council for seventeen years, being his mayoress in 1950–1, before she had to resign through ill health in 1952. Clara Abell was a magistrate, the founding president of Wakefield Business and Professional Women's Club and was elected as the national vice president of the National Association of Training Corps for Girls in 1945, aged 71. Clara Judge was assistant district commissioner for Wolf Cubs in Wakefield for twenty-one years, and well-known throughout the country for her work. In 1938 she was awarded the Scout Medal of Merit and ten years later received the bar to the medal.

Margaret Thomas became one of the first two women (with Fanny Stott) to be elected as aldermen on the council in 1938. In addition she was county borough organiser of the Wakefield WVS and honorary secretary of the Wakefield Women's Conservative Association. In the 1940s, feeling sorry for the old men who seemed to have nowhere to shelter in inclement weather except among the market stalls, she started a rest room at the WVS Northgate headquarters. It was the beginnings of the first Darby and Joan club in the country (although this may be disputed) and she played a leading role in the subsequent development of the movement. When awarded the MBE in the

1953 Coronation honours, she stated the award should be for the Wakefield WVS workers as a whole.

When Fanny Stott, by then of Grove House, 1, College Grove Rd, was elected as Wakefield's first female mayor, in November 1940, it was fifty years after her father, Joseph Haslegrave, had occupied the position. She was 58 years old and chose her recently married daughter Ida (known as Betty) Senior to be her mayoress. A very busy woman, Mrs Stott had qualified as a nurse in her teens and had been closely interested in hospital work, being on the Poor Law Hospital Committee and head of the Red Cross Hospital Supply Bandage Depot at the beginning of the war. Other committees she had served on included the St John's Home for Girls, the Victoria Nursing Association, the Clayton Hospital Ladies' Linen League, the West Riding Discharged Prisoners' Aid Society, and the Social Service Council. She was chairman of the Wakefield branch of the Civil and Nursing Reserve, vice president of the Wakefield Soroptomists' Club, president of the local branch of the College of Nursing, and president of the Wakefield Pontefract and Knottingley branch of the NSPCC, and on the board of governors of both the Wakefield Charities and the Wakefield Women's Conservative Association. At one time she had been president of the Wakefield women's section of the British Legion, and worked to set up a club for the wives of unemployed men.

As mayor, her first appeal was for a 'Penny Thank-Offering Scheme' whereby the residents of Wakefield were asked to place a penny into a family collecting box each night the city was free from air raids. By July 1941, when the fund was closed, more than £1,225 had been raised and sent to the Lord Mayor of London's central fund. In contrast with the blitz on London, bombs fell on Wakefield only one night during those seven months – the 14/15 March 1941, killing six people in Thornes Road.

Further fundraising and a little competition ensued when people in Britain rallied to the call to raise money for war weapons in a series of 'War Weapons Weeks' during 1941. Each town set targets of how much they wanted to raise, and Mrs Stott threw down her gauntlet, or rather her hat, to her male counterparts in other districts. Opening an exhibition of war photographs at Dewsbury Town Hall at the start of its 'War Weapons Week' in April, she referred to a friendly wager between herself and the mayor of Dewsbury, Mr Tom Myers:

> I am credibly informed, that rivalry between neighbouring towns is good publicity for War Weapons Weeks, and it was further to cement the ties of friendship between Wakefield and Dewsbury that I challenged Mr Myers a wager for a new hat on the results of our respective Weapons Week efforts. As Wakefield raised over one million pounds in February, and achieved £17 14s 9d per head of the population, you will appreciate your task not an easy one.

Her earlier, similar challenge to neighbouring Barnsley had been met with less approval by its mayor who declined the wager. The Methodist lay preacher said he appreciated the sporting spirit of the mayor of Wakefield but never at any time accepted wagers 'for either hats or halfpennies'.

Reports show Barnsley raised £14 5s 5d per head (£1m) and Dewsbury £21 12s per head (£1.1m). Nothing is recorded of whether anyone received a new hat.

When disaster struck at Crigglestone Colliery on 29 July 1941, Mrs Stott was quick to rally support for the dependants (eighteen widows and thirty-five children) of the twenty-two men killed in the explosion. She wrote to the *Yorkshire Post*, announcing the appeal fund, adding:

> As a woman I realise the deep grief and hardship which will fall upon the wives and families who have been left in straitened circumstances owing to the breadwinner having been rudely torn away. To calls for charitable purposes in the past I have had a handsome response, and, while I realise that the demands upon the private purse are exceptional, at the same time feel that the present appeal calls for no apology as all know the debt the country owes to the miners at the present time.

The fund closed at the end of December, when £8,503 had been raised. Regular weekly payments were made to the families of those affected by the tragedy.

When Effie Crowe, a former teacher, took her office as mayor four years later, the *Yorkshire Post and Leeds Intelligencer* noted that out of the 100 mayors of Wakefield, she was only the second woman to hold the position. Still, Bradford and Huddersfield were only just electing their first female mayors. Like Mrs Stott, Mrs Crowe too had family connections to the council – husband Tom was a fellow-alderman and had been mayor in 1937–8. Nor was she a stranger to public office having already been mayoress three times. She chose Mrs Winifred Ashton as her mayoress and husband Tom as deputy mayor. With the war over, her municipal work was perhaps less eventful than that of Fanny Stott. Two of her highlights were travelling to Wembley to witness Wakefield Trinity triumph at the Rugby League Cup Final in May 1946, and accompanying children from Flanshaw Lodge home on their day trip to Bridlington in August.

∞

Some Wakefield women had their political sights set higher than local government.

Even before women had the vote, they were politically active within the major parties. Wakefield had a Women's Unionist Association (which became the Wakefield Women's Conservative Association), before the First World War. Its president for almost forty years was Mrs Annie Hudson (née Gledhill) of Grove Hall, 60, College Grove, whose work for political and public services in Wakefield earned her the MBE in 1938 at the age of 72.

After women were granted the vote in 1918, the party restructured itself as the Women's Unionist Organisation, encompassing various groups, and worked hard to bring women into the political arena. Between 1921 and 1930 it published a magazine called *Home and Politics*. The WUO called for more education for women and requested speakers from Central Office, particularly in areas such as economics. Women travelled to the Conservative Party College for training, and study groups formed throughout the country, offering courses on everything from canvassing to foreign policy.[42] With women's interest in politics growing in Yorkshire, delegates from various constituencies gathered at quarterly meetings of the Yorkshire Federation of Women's Unionist Associations, often travelling long distances to attend. As well as a Wakefield association, there was also a Rothwell Division of the Women's Unionist Association, the boundaries of which included Walton and Chevet in Wakefield. Its chairman was Mrs Gwendoline Beaumont, sister-in-law of Florence, who, having been anti-suffrage prior to women having the vote, became politically active in 1918. She worked closely with Mrs Martha Kathleen Haslegrave (daughter of William Henry Kingswell of the Wakefield department store and sister-in-law of Fanny Stott), setting up the association and each taking it in turn to be president and chairman for a number of years. Mrs Beaumont was also a member of the Finance and General Purposes Committee of the Yorkshire Provincial Area and the Women's Advisory Council. Besides these senior organisations, she was president of the local Young Britons, and also took keen interest in the Junior Imperial League, a young men's Conservative group. On a more homely level she was vice-chairman of Woolley Church Council and vice-president of Woolley WI.

After her husband, Gerald Beaumont, (of Greaves, Atter and Beaumont solicitors) passed away in 1933, she turned her attention fully to politics. In October 1935, it was announced a woman candidate was to contest the 'far-flung constituency' of Rothwell for the first time. Gwendoline was the only woman among the National Party candidates standing. Her central campaign platform was for 'England' [sic] to show a united front to a distracted world, asserting that the National Government (a coalition formed in 1931 by Ramsay McDonald), having already proved its progressive policy, was worthy of the country's trust.

In a letter penned to the local press, her focus on the lives of women and children was also clear as she outlined her commitments to the electorate:

> [...] As a woman I know the value of family life, what our children mean to us, their health, their upbringing, their education and all the hopes we have for them. If elected I shall watch, with particular care all legislation which affects education, health, maternity welfare and the home. [...]

> [...] Living as I do in the midst of the West Yorkshire coalfields and realising the hazardous nature of the occupation, I know full well how the industry suffers today from the competition of other fuel, the many new inventions which adversely affect the use of coal, and the closing of foreign markets to our exports trade. I shall most strongly support the measures which the government are pressing forward to help the industry. The present position is unfair to all and must be ended. Strikes and lockouts only mean greater hardships for the women and children. [...]

> [...] I welcome the promise given by the government to raise, by a year, the school leaving age for those children for whom suitable employment cannot be found. I strongly hope that the extra year of education will be strictly practical for girls as well as boys. [...]

And although all three of her sons had been privately educated and gone up to Oxford (Stephen Gerald became a solicitor, Battle of Britain Spitfire pilot and deputy coroner in Wakefield; Herbert Christopher was a senior civil servant and secretary to the Radcliffe Commission during the Partition of India in 1947 and Robert Leslie was the youngest Fellow of Corpus Christi, Oxford and a tutor in ancient history, when he died as the result of a climbing accident in Wales in 1938, aged only 24), she recognised that these opportunities were not likely to come the way of the Rothwell population and added:

> [...] In these days of invention and research, far more attention ought to be given to the technical side of education, and I look forward to the granting of maintenance allowances for approved apprentices of promise. For a nation which has to maintain its standard of life by the scale and efficiency of its producers, we are perhaps paying too much attention to books and too little to the training and support of those will be the mechanics, research men, and inventors of the future. [...]

Reminding people it was their duty to vote, she urged all those who believed in a sane, ordered and progressive policy to record their vote for her.

It was a brave campaign. Rothwell was a staunch Labour constituency, and the incumbent MP, Mr William Lunn, had held the seat since 1918. Gwendoline spoke at every one of the thirty polling districts, but trying to convert a large working population, not in the least inclined to turn out to her meetings, required new techniques. Her canvassers pounced on people as they left their workplaces, they employed soap-box orators with voices that carried and they tried to round up audiences by door-knocking. Nobody said they weren't interested, but just hung out of windows and peered round their back doors, rather than stand out in the cold and wet. 'It's a pity we have no hecklers', complained one canvasser. 'They'd all come to hear someone heckled!'

Perhaps the good people of Rothwell couldn't bring themselves to heckle a lady. Described by a journalist as 'a middle-aged woman of great charm, simple, restrained, unaffected, with grey blue eyes and a fair girlish complexion, well-equipped for the weather in a neat tweed suit, dark brown hat, dark brown scarf and jumper and brogues', even the miners listened to her with utmost attention and courtesy.

With 10,000 extra voters in the constituency, there was a chance for the Conservatives to take the seat, however, a strong dislike for women candidates meant they were never going to vote for her. Later describing her enjoyable election experience, Gwendoline related how she'd often been told that a woman's place was in the home and that's where she ought to be. Even though she explained her family was grown up and she'd rather work than take up knitting, she could not convince them. That her campaign was doomed became apparent when she overheard one miner telling another, 'The only woman who could get in in this division is Mae West.'

With a seventy-five per cent turnout William Lunn increased his majority from 2,700 to 14,120. It was a landslide. Gwendoline acknowledged defeat, but said she was not downhearted.

With the outbreak of the Second World War there were no further general elections until July 1945, two months after VE Day, when Churchill's caretaker government was heavily defeated by the Labour party. Among those gaining one of the 242 new seats for Labour was Alice Martha Bacon, who beat the Conservative incumbent for Leeds North-East, John Craik-Henderson, by a majority of 8,464. She was the first Yorkshire woman to become an MP.

Alice was born in Normanton on 10 September 1909, daughter of Benjamin, a miner, and Charlotte (née Handley). The family lived with Charlotte's parents (who had moved to Yorkshire from Staffordshire in around 1890), at 346, Castleford Road. Described as an archetypal Yorkshire lass – tough, determined and warm of heart – like many clever working-class girls she aspired to more. She trained as a teacher and was still a school mistress in 1939. However, politics called and she was elected to the women's section of Labour's National Executive in 1941, one of the youngest to reach such a key position. A significant figure in the Labour movement she was practical and moderate in her approach. Her career as a Leeds MP continued until 1970, after which she entered the House of Lords as Baroness Bacon. Charity work, particularly for women's causes, interested her more than the Upper House and she raised money through concerts and other events. After Alice's retirement from the Commons none of the Leeds constituencies elected a woman MP until 2010 when Leeds West returned Rachel Reeves. More can be read about Alice Bacon in Rachel's book, *Alice in Westminster* (2016)

The struggle for women's recognition as capable politicians also continued in Wakefield. The Rothwell constituency (with its various boundary changes) remained a Labour seat until 2010. It has yet to return a woman MP. Wakefield, still under Labour, finally elected its first woman MP (Mary Creagh) in 2005.

CHAPTER SEVEN

Women's Progress in Wakefield

From the very beginning of the 100-year period covered by this book, women worked tirelessly to effect positive changes in the lives of other women. It had to be so. The men of Wakefield were busy, some in the thick of political work on behalf of Wakefield's citizens, some forging careers in trade or law, some running businesses and factories. Others simply worked long hours to provide food and shelter for their families. It was left to the women of Wakefield to take on the caring roles. Whether this was attending to life at home, nursing, teaching, fundraising, or looking after those who needed help, their work was vital and much went unrecorded.

It may seem rather stereotypical to cast women as being the carers, but there is no doubt they worked in different ways to the menfolk. Even those who later had the opportunity to build careers or push for changes, did so collaboratively with other women.

When the Wakefield Business and Professional Women's Club was established in around 1943, it presented women from various organisations in the city with the chance to network, to learn about each other's working lives and to use their wide range of experience collectively to move or support resolutions that affected their lives. Membership wasn't large, but consisted of a diverse group of hardworking, enthusiastic women. It included the Misses Avison – Vera a butcher's clerk and Annie, headmistress of an elementary school – whose two brothers ran the family businesses of butcher and wholesale confectioner,

Miss F.E. Oesterlein (presumed of the butchers' family), Miss Annie M. Clarke, nursing and midwife inspector, Miss Elsie Julia Nicholson, shorthand typist, Mrs Ada B. Clayton, shorthand typist at an auto-engineers, Mrs Frances E. Crosby, whose husband ran an auto-engineering business (so perhaps Ada worked for him), Miss Ethel Clinker, a parlour maid at Chevet Hall and Mrs Clara Abell, magistrate and councillor.

They met fortnightly at 2, South Parade, the home at the time of the Avisons, and invited guests to speak, usually about their working lives, which they could then discuss. One of the early speakers, in July 1944, was the mayor of Wakefield, Councillor Hopkins. He divulged the work of the various committees and sub-committees, post-war plans for a new abattoir, market hall and public conveniences and welcomed forthright questions on why there were only four women on the council and why only women with educational experience could be members of the education committee. The ladies accepted his invitation and attended a council meeting on 5 September. Other speakers told of their roles running district nursing, working with juvenile offenders in the probation service, occupational therapy, work among Anglo-Indian children, printing and book-binding and magazine editing.[43]

Despite women being taken more seriously, their appearance was still judged and commented on. Maybe for this reason the club thought it pertinent to invite Muriel Smith to speak about 'hairdressing for business and professional women'. Pointing out that the majority of women did not make the most of themselves with regard to the care of their hair – a woman's 'crowning glory' – Muriel demonstrated a simple hairstyle, which, she said, 'was quite easy to manage'. According to club minutes, the number of questions asked showed members did intend to pay more attention to the care and style of their hair in the future, but there's a nuance that the advice wasn't entirely welcomed!

The interests of the Wakefield Business and Professional Women's Club (BPWC) extended further than the local district. As part of the International Federation of Business and

Professional Women, founded in Geneva in 1930, its official aims and ambitions were for 'each woman, as a citizen, to bring to the national policy of her own country, the contribution of forward-looking and constructive thought followed by determined action, and for each woman to dedicate herself to protect and promote the interests of all other women in business and the professions'. This effort made in developing women's professional and leadership potential at all levels was intended to lead to the equal participation of women and men in power and decision-making roles.[44]

Wakefield's BPWC held 'friendship evenings', inviting women from clubs in other towns to attend. That these were events organised by women is evident from the detailed planning that took place. Meeting rooms, to accommodate around 150 guests, were decorated with flowers. Refreshments were provided and small tables were arranged in a way that was conducive to chat. The club's minute book reveals:

> Miss Osterlein would provide ready-made sandwiches and Miss Avison offered to provide sufficient bridge rolls for everyone to have one each. It was thought these could be filled with savoury or sweet and several members said they would make suitable fillings. Offers of cakes were also made.

The friendship meetings included an informative, topical talk, followed by a singing recital and a recitation, then supper, with further entertainment afterwards. Bonds were formed with women of other districts and each club knew it could call on another for discussion and support of resolutions they proposed to put to the government.

Between 1944 and 1950 these included:

> That the National Federation of Business and Professional Women's clubs strongly protest against the non-recognition in full of British women war-correspondents. We demand their recognition without

restriction other than those which might be imposed on their men colleagues for security reasons, so they may properly fulfil their duty to the British public.

That this convention views with grave concern HM Treasury's declaration on oral evidence before the Royal Commission on equal pay, that if at any time the percentage of women in administrative roles [in the Civil Service] rose to something of the order of 20-25% it might be necessary to impose artificial barriers on the entry of women to this grade by the reservation of a guaranteed percentage of vacancies to men, and proposes that the Executive Committee approach the government with a view to ascertaining that in all circumstances the principle of equal entry into the Civil Service by competitive examination (which has been in operation since 1925) should be adhered to.

That public libraries to be open on Sunday afternoons and evenings so they may be used by working men and women. They could, if necessary, be shut some other day as in Paris.

To ask the minister of education to review the serious position of the growing tendency of local education authorities to appoint men as headteachers of schools which have been amalgamated into mixed departments. The post should be given on experience and ability and not on sex alone and local authorities should advertise the post impartially so women teachers might not be penalised on account of their sex.

To amend the Finance Act with regard to income tax so that women could receive post-war credits on their own account and without the joint application for apportionment from husband and wife. [Women who had put their maximum effort into the war should not now be subject to this injustice it was argued.]

> To strongly urge the government to issue, without delay,
> a form of birth certificate for general purposes which
> would not disclose illegitimacy. [The case was that it
> would end injustice of a lifelong humiliation.]

Club members were also canvassed for their opinions on topics
that affected women and within a twelve-month period from
1944 they'd discussed issues such as:

- The desirability of equal pay for equal work and the various
  differing rates prevailing.
- Extending shop opening hours to allow women to buy
  groceries after work.
- Introducing a clause in the national insurance scheme,
  entitling spinsters to a pension at 55 instead of 60 and,
- With regard to the removal of marriage bars to employment,
  the suitability of women with young families working when
  it would fall to single women to bear the brunt of the
  married ones' leaves of absence which were inevitable to her
  circumstances.

One of the key achievements of the International Federation
of Business and Professional Women was its gaining of
consultative status with the United Nations in 1947, soon after
the UN was established. It is indicative of the fact that women
were now far more involved and had more influence in political
affairs. A pamphlet, 'Women and the UNO' was circulated
from the BPWC headquarters to all clubs in September 1947,
and Wakefield formed a subcommittee under Annie Clarke
to study its contents and report back. A speaker was invited
from the United Nations Association to explain its origins and
purpose and relationship to the United Nations Organisation.
His appeal for the Wakefield club's support for UNO through
the medium of UNA resulted in the club joining the UNA as a
corporate member in November 1947.

Yet alongside national and global affairs, the ladies of the
Wakefield club still found great pleasure in the more homely
things in life. One member who definitely brought joy to the

club's affairs was Miss Ethel Clinker, one of only two staff remaining at Chevet Hall. Her job as a servant might not have qualified her as a 'business and professional woman', but she introduced valuable and enthusiastic fundraising skills to the group. It is easy to imagine the ladies' delight when Ethel invited them to visit the hall and park, where she would make tea and take a collection for the club funds. It would be the last opportunity for most to see the house in its glory, before the fixtures and fittings were dismantled and the estate later sold to Wakefield Council. The club's minute book reveals, with some amusement, that ample justice was done to the full Yorkshire tea – set out in the conservatory – especially by certain officers who, having been lost in the woods, climbed several fences before finally arriving at their destination. It was a very happy evening, long-remembered. Another charming money-making ruse was conjured up by Ethel, who, with her employer Sir Arthur Pilkington's permission, picked and bunched a huge quantity of daffodils in the park, and presented them to the club. The minutes report the basket was 'swiftly emptied', raising over thirty-five shillings in the process.[45]

Raising money for club funds was always necessary and in a similar fashion, Mrs Bracewell brought a batch of her homemade biscuits for members to enjoy with their customary cup of tea at the close of meetings – and sold the recipe for 3d each.

The shared camaraderie of being with a group of women was embodied in the numerous days out and regular dinners in the immediate post-war period. It wasn't always straightforward. Fuel and food was still rationed, so planning a coach trip or a restaurant meal had to be done well in advance. It was over a year after VE Day before the club managed its 'victory dinner' – a day trip to Scarborough by coach with lunch and tea at Rowntree's café on the esplanade, but this was soon followed up by a New Year dinner at the Three Houses at Sandal, an afternoon trip to Burnsall with tea at the Red Lion, and a trip to Saltburn, returning via Bridlington and Sewerby Park after lunch at the Zetland Hotel.[46]

After the struggles of the past hundred years, these happy women may have sensed their lives were on the cusp of change. They were making their voices heard and many had more independence, money, courage, and choice. But others still had a long way to go.

Notes

1. West Yorkshire Archive Service, *House of Recovery Annual Report* 1852

2. Histpop.org

3. William White, *History, Gazetteer, and Directory, of the West-Riding of Yorkshire, with the city of York and port of Hull*

4. Wakefield Local Studies Library, *Wakefield Council education committee minutes*

5. Wakefield Local Studies Library, *Thornes House, Story of a School*, Nora J. George

6. Slater's *Royal National Commercial Directory of the Northern Counties 1855, Vol 1 (Durham, Northumberland, and Yorkshire Royal National Commercial Directory)*

7. Sugden family scrapbook

8. E. Green's Company History, *Waste Not*

9. Wakefield Local Studies Library, *Wakefield Express* 8 February 2008

10. Wakefield Local Studies Library, *Wakefield Express (no date)*

11. Wakefield Local Studies Library, *Wakefield Council Minutes* 1941–45

12. Burdett, *Register of Nurses 1898*

13. Burdett, *Register of Nurses 1905*

14. Ibid

15. *The London Gazette* 5 August 1919

16. Wakefield Local Studies Library, *Wakefield Council Minutes 1906*

17. Wakefield Grammar School In 1914, *Wakefield Girls' High School and the War Years*

18. Ibid

19. King's College London Online Exhibition, Chelsea College

20. British Newspaper Archives, *Nottingham Evening Post*

21. British Newspaper Archives, *Yorkshire Post and Leeds Intelligencer*

22. West Yorkshire Archive Service, *Colin Jackson, Wakefield Constabulary 1848–1968*

23. Ibid

24. Wakefield Local Studies Library, *Notes on Public Health in Wakefield during the 19th Century and from 1901 to 1935, Dr Thomas Gibson, Wakefield Medical Officer of Health*

25. Ibid

26. Ibid

27. Kate Taylor (ed.), *Aspects of Wakefield*

28. Wakefield Local Studies Library, *Notes on Public Health in Wakefield during the 19th Century and from 1901 to 1935, Dr Thomas Gibson, Wakefield Medical Officer of Health*

29. *The Women's Suffrage Movement: A Reference Guide 1866–1928* By Elizabeth Crawford

30. West Yorkshire Archive Service, *West Riding Industrial School Annual Report 1894*

31. West Yorkshire Archive Service, *West Riding Industrial School 37th Annual Report 1902*

32. West Yorkshire Archive Service, *Industrial Home For Discharged Female Prisoners, Register Of Girls, 1885–1901*

33. West Yorkshire Archive Service, *Mothers' Union Minutes 1895–2001* (1896)

34. West Yorkshire Archive Service, *Mothers' Union Minutes 1895–2001* (1915)

35. West Yorkshire Archive Service, *Co-operative Women's Guild Minutes 1908-85 (1910)*

36. British Newspaper Archives, *Common Cause* reports (various)

37. Ibid

38. British Newspaper Archives, *Common Cause* June 1913, clothing advertisement

39. British Newspaper Archives, *Common Cause 1914*

40. Wakefield Grammar School In 1914, Wakefield Girls' High School and the War Years

41. Wakefield Local Studies Library, *Wakefield Council Minutes 1938-50*

42. Bodleian Library, Oxford, Archives and manuscripts, Conservative women after suffrage

43. West Yorkshire Archive Service, *Wakefield Business And Professional Women's Club Records 1943–50*

44. International Federation of Business and Professional Women website

45. West Yorkshire Archive Service, *Wakefield Business And Professional Women's Club Records 1943–50*

46. Ibid

Wakefield Prison Female Staff

Year	Name	Occupation	Age	Born	Place of Birth
1851	Mary Ann Crossland	Matron	52	1799	Bishop Monkton, Yorkshire
1851	Mary Flockton	Matron	53	1798	Middleton, Yorkshire
1851	Sarah Johnson	Matron	35	1816	Bishop Monkton, Yorkshire
1851	Zillah Paige	Matron	37	1814	Ripon, Yorkshire
1851	Jane Shepherd	Matron	67	1784	Northallerton, Yorkshire
1851	Mary A. Whitfield	Matron	34	1817	Stanley, Yorkshire
1861	Elizabeth Love	Matron	37	1824	Sheffield, Yorkshire
1861	Sarah Binns	Assistant Matron	34	1827	Ripon, Yorkshire
1861	Mary Ann Crossland	Assistant Matron	62	1799	Bishop Monkton, Yorkshire
1861	Mary Flockton	Assistant Matron	63	1798	Middleton, Yorkshire
1861	Sarah Johnson	Assistant Matron	45	1816	Wakefield, Yorkshire
1861	Martha Shaw	Assistant Matron	35	1826	Wakefield, Yorkshire

1861	Elizabeth Whiteley	Assistant Matron	29	1832	Warmsworth, Yorkshire
1871	Elizabeth Love	Matron	47	1825	Sheffield, Yorkshire
1871	Sarah Binns	Deputy Matron	44	1827	Ripon, Yorkshire
1871	Martha Shaw	Infirmary Matron	45	1826	Wakefield, Yorkshire
1871	Anne Broomhead	Assistant Matron	35	1836	Rothwell, Yorkshire
1871	Sarah Burnley	Assistant Matron	58	1813	Ripon, Yorkshire
1871	Arabella Hawley	Assistant Matron	33	1838	Rotherham, Yorkshire
1871	Susan Parkinson	Assistant Matron	41	1830	Bradford, Yorkshire
1871	Eliza Pearson	Assistant Matron	43	1828	Wakefield, Yorkshire
1871	Hannah Maria Tyas	Assistant Matron	49	1822	Wakefield, Yorkshire
1871	Ann Atkinson	Gate Porter	65	1806	Wakefield, Yorkshire
1871	Mary Ann Crosland	Gate Porter	72	1799	Ripon, Yorkshire
1881	Caroline Mascon	Principal Warder	47	1834	Farnley, Yorkshire
1881	Jane Jones	Prison Hospital Nurse	38	1843	London, Middlesex
1881	Ann Kenyon	Prison Hospital Nurse	52	1829	Ferrybridge, Yorkshire
1881	Elizabeth Berry	Prison Warder	35	1846	Pinxton, Derbyshire
1881	Ann Jackinson	Prison Warder	40	1841	Huddersfield, Yorkshire
1881	Elizabeth Senior	Prison Warder	53	1828	Halifax, Yorkshire
1881	Ellen Ward	Prison Warder	41	1840	Wakefield, Yorkshire

1881	Mary Alice Wilby	Prison Warder	29	1852	Ossett, Yorkshire
1891	Elizabeth Flockton	Matron	54	1837	Wakefield, Yorkshire
1891	Jane Jones	Warder	48	1843	London
1891	Ann Kenyon	Warder	62	1829	Ferrybridge, Yorkshire
1891	Mary E Pendlebury	Warder	25	1866	Newton Heath, Lancashire
1891	Elizabeth Senior	Warder	63	1828	Halifax, Yorkshire
1891	Sarah Ann Walton	Warder	48	1843	Wetherby, Yorkshire
1891	Ann Whitaker	Warder	55	1836	Horsforth, Yorkshire
1901	Sarah Bellinger	Chief Matron	45	1856	West Woodhay, London
1901	Elizabeth Cartwright	Principal Warder	40	1861	Clapham, Yorkshire
1901	Kate Goundwell	Schoolmistress Warder	32	1869	Gildersome, Yorkshire
1901	Phoebe Collis	Female Warder	29	1872	Kirby Stephen, Westmorland
1901	Emma Cooling	Female Warder	30	1871	Gosport, Hampshire
1901	Charlotte Dyer	Female Warder	30	1871	Portsmouth, Hampshire
1901	Mary Galloway	Female Warder	31	1870	Wakefield, Yorkshire
1901	Miriam Hardman	Female Warder	24	1877	Wakefield, Yorkshire
1901	Laura Henny	Female Warder	24	1877	Pitminster, Somerset
1901	Mary Lewis	Female Warder	24	1877	Mydrim, Carmarthenshire
1901	Rachel Maltley	Female Warder	40	1861	Leeds, Yorkshire
1901	Sillie Wainman	Female Warder	28	1873	Preston, Lancashire

Wartime Nurseries Staff

Burneytops
Matrons

- Miss Lillian Green of Sharlston, temporary resident matron, 19 August 1942 to 10 March 1943, at £130
- Mrs G.H. Field of Wakefield, deputy matron, 9 August 1942 to 10 September 1943, at £160, rising by annual increments of £10
- Mrs H. Griffiths acting deputy matron, 25 March to 23 April 1943 at £160
- Miss Florence Mailing of Preston as resident deputy matron at £110 or £160 if non-resident
- Eileen Mosley of Wakefield, resident matron, 7 January 1944 at £140
- Mrs M.A. Taylor temporary matron, January 1943 to 2 July 1943
- Miss Ellen Martin of Storrington in Sussex, temporary matron

Others

- Mrs Mary Fisher, assistant nurse, 1 January 1943 at £120
- Miss Rosemary Smith of Hemsworth temporary non-resident certificated nursery trained nurse at £135, took up residence at the nursery on the 1 July 1942 and in consequence her salary was adjusted to £95 rising by annual increments of £5 to £110
- Miss Marie Hauxwell, 3 April to June 1943, nursery assistant £120

- Mrs Edith Nadon, 29 November 1943, nursery assistant at £135
- Mrs Ann B. Kelly, resident nursing assistant from 19 October 1942 at £80
- Miss Emily Rothwell, resident nursing assistant from 19 October 1942 at £80
- Miss Mabel Johnson, resident nursing assistant from 19 October 1942 to 7 July 1943 at £80

- Mrs Mary K. Holgate, Wakefield, probationer nurse
- Miss Patricia Holland, Wakefield, probationer nurse to 17 September 1942
- Mavis L. Holmes, Wakefield, probationer nurse
- Miss Sybil Howell, Outwood, probationer nurse
- Miss Joan Lumb, Heath, probationer nurse
- Shirley M. Cawthraw, Wakefield, probationer nurse
- Mary E. Dodding, Wakefield, probationer nurse
- Miss Dorothy Moorhouse, resident probationer nurse from 5 October 1942

Probationer nurses all paid £52 (£26 if residential)

- Mrs Schofield, cook to 12 December 1942
- Miss F.E. Pierpoint, temporary cook, 14 December 1942 at £90
- Mrs Jessica Braley of Normanton, non-resident cook, 30 April 1943 for probation period of a month
- Mrs Amelia Wilde, part-time domestic help, 23 December 1942 to 7 April 1943 at 1*s* and 1*d* per hour
- Mrs Wilshaw, cleaner, 31 March 1943 at 1s and 1d per hour
- Mrs Philpott, cleaner, 5 April 1943, then cook from 2 September 1943
- Mrs Neilson, laundress, 7 April to 25 June 1943
- Mrs Radcliffe of Wakefield, daily cleaner
- Mrs l. Simmister, cleaner to 24 March 1943
- Miss Becquet, temporary cleaner at 1s 1d per hour
- Mrs Goodsell Brookhill, Chevet Lane, Sandal, voluntary work from 9 February 1943
- Miss Crabtree, 18 Clement Street, Wakefield, voluntary work from 9 February 1943

Lupset
Matrons
- Mrs Ena Crayford of Wakefield, temporary non-resident matron 19 August 1942 to 31 March 1943
- Mrs Caines, deputy matron at £160
- Mrs P. Bellamy of Holmfirth, matron, June 1943 to 30 June 1944
- Mrs B. Bessant of Leeds, matron at £230 rising by annual increments of £10 (less £25 per year in respect of meals)

Others
- Miss A.J. Greenhalgh, nursery nurse, 25 January 1943 at £135 rising by annual increments of £5
- Mrs Marjorie Keynes of Wakefield, temporary non-resident nursery nurse £135
- Joan Hodgson, nursery nurse, March 1944 at £150
- Mrs E. Maiden, nursery assistant to 29 May 1944
- Mrs S.M. Cooke, nursery assistant
- Mrs M. Robinson, nursery assistant
- Miss Norton, nursery assistant, 1 January 1943 at £120
- J.E. Lumb, nursery assistant

- Miss June Walshaw, probationer nurse 21 June 1943
- Beryl Lockwood, Wakefield, probationer nurse
- Miss Molly Walton, Wakefield, probationer nurse

- Miss G.A. Norton, Wakefield, temporary non-resident cook at £90
- Mrs G. Gladwin, cook, 4 January 1943 at £90
- Miss A. Westle, cook, June to 26 August 1943
- Mrs Cooper, temporary cook, 27 August to 1 September, then cleaner

- Mrs M. Wade, Wakefield, daily cleaner to 24 March 1943
- Miss F. Gott, domestic staff
- Mrs M.E. Taylor, domestic staff
- Mrs A.I. Warrington, domestic staff
- Mrs D. Rowley, laundress, 30 June 1943

Wakefield's Voluntary Aid Detachment

From 1914–18, Wakefield had two auxiliary military hospitals, Park Lane Auxiliary Military Hospital (also known as White Rose) and St John's Auxiliary Military Hospital, Wentworth House, which was preceded by Clayton Hospital. These are noted throughout this appendix as Park Lane and St John's.

1. Miss Clarice Abbishaw, 12 Ashfield Terrace, Thorpe, Wakefield and 4 Cliff Terrace, Robin Hood, Wakefield. Age when engaged: 24. Served as a nurse, paid £2 10s a week, at 2nd North General Hospital, Leeds (Beckett's Park) from 27 June 1916 to 11 November 1918. Transferred to 10th General Hospital, St Adrian, France to 8 July 1919.
2. Miss Annis Alack, 2h Ingwell St, Wakefield. Served for 500 hours part-time nursing duties on wards at Park Lane from May 1918.
3. Miss Dorothy Atkinson, Manygates Park, Sandal, Wakefield. Served 2,732 hours as a nursing sister (& canteen duties) at St John's from 1 November 1916 to 28 February 1919.
4. Miss Elizabeth Austwick, 27 Regent St, New Scarborough, Wakefield. Served 2,500 hours of nursing duties at Park Lane from 1 September 1917.
5. Miss Evelyn Bagnall, 44 Mt Clay Terrace, Eastmoor Rd, Wakefield.

Served 160 hours of ward duties at Park Lane from
November 1918.

6. Miss Lily Beaumont, Highfield, Hunsworth, Wakefield.
    Served 704 hours as a kitchen maid from 7 June 1918 to
    29 January 1919.

7. Mrs Rachel Bedford, Yorkshire Buildings, Wood St,
    Wakefield.
    Served 754 hours as a nursing sister at St John's from
    16 March 1911 to 28 February 1919.

8. Miss Lily Bendall, Station Road, Hemsworth, Wakefield.
    Served for 77 hours of housework at Darrington Auxiliary
    Military Hospital, Pontefract between 2 and 9 June 1917.

9. Miss E.M. Betts, Ivy House, Kinsley, Wakefield.
    Served 517 hours as a nurse between 4 August 1917 and
    6 January 1918.

10. Mrs Mabel Blakey (nee Taylor), Milnthorpe, nr Wakefield.
    Served 1,288 hours as a nursing sister at St John's from
    12 April 1915 to 28 February 1919.

11. Miss Edith Blenkinsopp, Savile St, Wakefield.
    Served 756 hours as a nursing sister at St John's from
    26 December 1913 to 28 February 1919.

12. Gertrude Bradley, 19 Smyth St, Wakefield.
    Served 100 hours of secretarial work at White Rose
    Hospital, from 14 July 1918

13. Miss Celia Irene Maude Bramley, Outwood Hall,
    Wakefield.
    Age when engaged: 24. Served as full-time nurse at Furness
    Auxiliary Hospital, Harrogate from 13 June 1918 to
    27 September 1918.

14. Miss Ida Olga Mary Moorhouse Bramley, Outwood Hall,
    Wakefield.
    Age when engaged: 27. Served as a nurse at Bath Military
    Hospital from 11 April 1917 to 11 May 1917; St John's
    Hall, Sevenoaks from 15 May 1917 to August 1917, and at
    Furness Auxiliary Hospital, Harrogate from 28 February
    1918 to 30 March 1919.

15. Miss Muriel Donna C. Bramley, Outwood Hall, Wakefield.
    Served at St John's Auxiliary Hospital, Sevenoaks
    from 3 March 1917 to 9 August 1917 and at Furness

Auxiliary Hospital, Harrogate from 28 February 1918 to 27 December 1918.

16. Mrs Mildred May Bramley Taylor, Hemsworth Lane Ends, Hemsworth, Wakefield.
    Served as Ward Sister at Darrington Auxiliary Military Hospital, Pontefract from 19 February 1915 and 2,310 hours as Sister in Charge at Stapleton Park Hospital, Pontefract from 31 May 1917.

17. Miss Barbara Briggs, Beechfield, Sandal, Wakefield.
    Served 2,863 hours of canteen duties at St John's from 27 May 1918.

18. Miss Dorothy Briggs, The Cliffe, Sandal, Wakefield.
    Served 8,265 hours as a nursing sister with quartermaster's duties at St John's from 10 April 1915 to 28 February 1919.

19. Miss Marjorie E.B. Briggs, The Cliffe, Sandal, Wakefield.
    Served 2,854 hours as a nursing sister with canteen duties at St John's from 5 May 1915 to 28 February 1919.

20. Miss Phyllis Mary Bywater, The Vicarage, Outwood, Wakefield.
    Served 504 hours as secretary (although was also a nursing sister) at St John's from 17 August 1918 to 28 February 1919.

21. Mrs Mabel Cameron (née Gloyne), Arundel Street, Wakefield.
    Served 1,162 hours as a nursing sister at St John's, from 17 October 1910 (joined VAD) to 28 February 1919.

22. Miss Florence Mary Carter, Oak Lodge, Chigwell, Essex
    Served 2,618 hours as a nursing sister at St John's, from 6 May 1917 to 28 February 1919.

23. Miss Chappell, Marsh Farm, Kinsley, Wakefield.
    Served 737 hours as probationer nurse then as cook at Stapleton Park Hospital, Pontefract.

24. Miss Maggie Charlesworth, 5 Addingford, Horbury, Wakefield.
    Age when engaged: 23. Served at Ripon Military Hospital from 8 August 1916 and Military Hospital in France from 18 September 1918 to 16 March 1919.

25. Miss Helen Stanley Clark, 5 St John's Square, Wakefield.

Age when engaged: 35¼. Served as cook, paid £40 a year, at Netley Military Hospital, Southampton from September 1915 to February 1916 and as cook in charge of Red Cross and kitchen in Salonika (£50 a year) from 28 May 1917 to 7 September 1918 and at Westbourne Hospital, 55, Porchester Terrace, London from 29 October 1918 to 1 December 1918.

Of excellent character she earned very good reports as a capable earnest worker. Left Salonika to go on leave to England, but after her departure a cable was sent to London advising the closure of her contract, as owing to deafness and malaria, it was not thought wise to allow her to return to Salonika.

26. Miss Ruby Cockburn, Grove Road, Horbury, Wakefield.
    Age when engaged: 30. Served as a Sister (paid 1 guinea a week) from 6 October 1914 until 19 January 1919 at various overseas hospitals viz: No. 13 General Hospital, No. 7 General Hospital (known as Malassises Hospital), St Omer; No. 2 British Red Cross Hospital, Rouen; No. 5 British Red Cross Hospital, Wimereux; No.16 A Train; No. 8 Le Touquet; No 8. Boulogne.
    Was awarded 1914 Star and Royal Red Cross 2nd Class.

27. Mrs Mary Collier, Beech House, St John's, Wakefield.
    Served 910 hours as a nursing sister at St John's, from 7 July 1918 to 28 February 1919.

28. Miss Sarah Maria Cormack, 7 Brooklyn Terrace, Newton Hill, Wakefield.
    Age when engaged: 52. Served as a clerk at East Leeds War Hospital from 19 April 1916 to 17 June 1919.

29. Miss Annie Elizabeth Couldwell, 88 Thornes Lane, Wakefield.
    Age when engaged: 26. Served as a nurse at Leeds 2nd North (Beckett's Park) from 28 April 1915 to 28 November 1917 and at Liverpool 1st West General Hospital from 1 December 1917 to 10 April 1919.

30. Miss Annie Couldwell, c/o St John's Auxiliary Military Hospital, Wentworth House, Wakefield.
    Served as a nursing sister paid £30 per year at St John's from 30 March 1915 for two years.

31. Miss Margaret Creaser, Westgate, Wakefield.
Served 1,000 hours nursing and ward work at Park Lane,
from May 1918.

32. Miss Mary C. Eden, The Manor House, Heath, Wakefield.
Served 3,199 hours as a nursing sister at St John's, from
28 January 1917 to 28 February 1919.

33. Miss Cecilia Elstone, Kinsley Hotel, Kinsley, Wakefield.
Served 792 hours as cook both on the front and at
Darrington Auxiliary Hospital, Pontefract from 12 June
1917 to 21 November 1918.

34. Miss Mary Fallas, 34 Northgate, Wakefield.
Served full-time doing office work and nursing duties at
Park Lane, from 7 May 1917
Honours awarded: Service 13 months stripe.

35. Miss Winifred Annie Fishenden, Gordon Lodge, Glenluce
Rd, Blackheath, London
Served 3,220 hours as a nursing sister at St John's from
12 November 1917 to June 1919.

36. Miss Catherine Mary Fisher, Park House, South Kirkby
Road, Wakefield.
Age when engaged: 46 years. Served as trained nurse
paid 1 guinea week from 20 April 1917 to 5 January 1919
(pay at termination £1 4s 10d a week).

37. Miss Madge Fitton, Halcliffe House, Horbury, Wakefield.
Served 485 hours in recreation room duties at St John's
from 5 November 1918 to 28 February 1919.

38. Miss Mary Frobisher, 10 Hatfeild Street, Wakefield.
Served 4,070 hours as a nursing sister and quartermaster's
deputy at St John's from 17 December 1910 (joined VAD)
to 28 February 1919.

39. Miss Mary Alice Hunt Garnett, Heath Common, Wakefield.
Served 2,863 hours of canteen duties at St John's from
June 1917 to February 1919.

40. Miss Edna Gascoigne, Castle Road, Sandal, Nr Wakefield.
Served as full-time nurse at Park Lane and St John's from
May 1917 to November 1918.

41. Lady Constance Milnes-Gaskell, Thornes House, Wakefield.
Served intermittently for total of twenty-seven months as
Commandant between 5 August 1914 and December 1917

at hospitals in London. Awarded Lady of Justice Order of St John.

42. Miss Lillian Henderson Gledhill, 21 Little Westgate, Wakefield.
    Served 2,683 hours of canteen duties at St John's, from 5 May 1917 to February 1919.

43. Miss Annie Gloyne, 4 Arundel Street, Wakefield.
    Served 652 hours as a nursing sister at St John's from 17 December 1910 (joined VAD) to 28 February 1919.

44. Miss Constance Gloyne, 4 Arundel Street, Wakefield.
    Age when engaged: 25. Served 780 hours as nurse at St John's plus Military Hospital in France from 28 September 1915 to 19 February 1917 and Tidworth Military Hospital, Wiltshire to February 1919.
    Mentioned in Despatches on 17 April 1919.

45. Mrs Alice M. Graham, Horbury Road, Wakefield.
    Served 3,069 hours as a nursing sister at St John's from 28 March 1916 to 28 February 1919.

46. Miss Mabel Green, Beech Holme, Outwood Wakefield.
    Served 3,108 hours as Assistant Quartermaster at St John's from 6 May 1917 to 28 February 1919.

47. Miss Gertrude Haley, Highfield, Sandal Wakefield.
    Served as full-time Quartermaster VAD at White Rose Auxiliary Military Hospital, Wakefield from July 1918.

48. Miss Nellie Hall, 179 Alverthorpe Rd, Wakefield.
    Served 310 hours as nurse at Park Lane from May 1918.

49. Miss Susan Hall, Crigglestone near Wakefield.
    Age when engaged: 34. Served as a sister at Queen Alexandra Hospital, Malo-les-Bains, Dunkirk, France from 24 February 1915 to 6 November 1915.
    Awarded 1915 Star.

50. Miss Eliza Hampshire, South Lane, Netherton, Nr Wakefield.
    Served 840 hours as a nursing sister at St John's from 26 January 1911 (joined VAD) to 28 February 1919.

51. Miss Ellen Hawkins, 5 Hague Terrace, Hemsworth, Wakefield.
    Age when engaged: 28. Served as 'house member' from 7 October 1917 to 7 February 1919.

52. Miss Eva Hawksworth, Clarendon Street, Wakefield
    Served 8,602 hours as a nursing sister at St John's from
    12 March 1913 (joined VAD) to 28 February 1919.
53. Miss Edith Hey, Roslyn Villa, Hemsworth, Wakefield.
    Served 110 hours as a housemaid at Darrington Auxiliary
    Military Hospital, Pontefract from 2 June 1917 to
    1 October 1917.
54. Miss Margaret Hodgson, Glaslyn, Agbrigg Rd, Sandal,
    Wakefield.
    Age when engaged: 30. Served as a nursing sister paid £30
    a year at St John's and Kinmel Military Camp, Wales from
    4 June 1917 to 4 July 1919.
55. Miss Nellie Hopkinson, Low Hall Farm, Hemsworth,
    Wakefield.
    Served for 704 hours working in the wards at Darrington
    Auxiliary Military Hospital, Pontefract from 26 June 1917
    to 29 January 1919.
56. Miss Helen Barbara Howard Hall, 10, South Parade,
    Wakefield.
    Served 2,910 hours as a nursing sister at St John's from
    30 May 1917 to 28 February 1919.
57. Miss Jessie Howlett, Holgate Lodge, Hemsworth,
    Wakefield.
    Served 1,201 hours as a parlour maid and cook at
    Stapleton Park Hospital, Pontefract from 31 August 1915
    to 19 November 1918.
58. Miss Ruth Howlett, Holgate Lodge, Hemsworth,
    Wakefield.
    Age when engaged: 32. Served as a nurse at Derbyshire
    Royal Infirmary and at a Military Hospital in France from
    12 October 1915 to 29 August 1919. Awarded Royal Red
    Cross 2nd Class on 1 January 1918 and 1915 Star.
59. Mrs Agnes Hoyle, 24 Plumpton St, Wakefield.
    Served 162 hours nursing duties at Park Lane, Wakefield
    from 24 September 1918.
60. Mrs Ada Louisa Jackson, 25 Westfield Road, Hemsworth,
    Wakefield.
    Served 121 hours as a cook as Darrington Auxiliary
    Military Hospital, Pontefract `between 8 and 19 April 1918.

61. Miss Eva Jackson, Clayton Hospital, Wakefield.
Served 776 hours of general work at Duncombe Park
Hospital, Helmsley from September 1917 to January 1919.

62. Miss Marjorie Jackson, c/o Supt Jackson, Wood St,
Wakefield.
Served 552 hours of pantry work at White Rose Auxiliary
Military Hospital, Wakefield from July 1918.

63. Miss Florence Emily Jenkins, Electric Cottages, Nostell,
Wakefield.
Age when engaged: 23. Served as a nurse at 2nd West
General Hospital, Manchester from 9 October 1916 to
8 November 1916.

64. Mrs Clara B. Judge, Southgate, Wakefield.
Served 588 hours as a nursing sister at St John's, from
14 August 1914 to 28 February 1919.

65. Mademoiselle Marthe Junod, (Mrs McBurney), St John's
Square Wakefield.
Served 158 hours gathering, picking and drying moss
and knitting and sewing etc. from November 1917 to
November 1918.

66. Mrs Nellie King, Belgrave Mount, Pinderfields, Wakefield.
Resident Commandant of Clayton VAD and St John's
Auxiliary Military Hospitals Wakefield from August 1914
to February 1919.
Awarded Royal Red Cross 2nd Class.

67. Mr Tom King, Belgrave Mount, Pinderfields, Wakefield.
Served 3,500 hours as Hon. Secretary and Transport
Officer for St John's, from August 1914

68. Miss Evelyn Louisa Lampen (Mrs Ferguson), Pledwick
House, Wakefield.
Age when engaged: 29 years. Served as a trained nurse paid
a guinea a week, in various hospitals in France and Egypt,
including No. 1 Red Cross Hospital, No. 8 Red Cross
Hospital, No. 2 Red Cross Hospital, Rouen, from 24 May
1916 to 6 January 1919.

69. Miss Dorothy Leatham, Hemsworth Hall, Wakefield.
Served 2,224 hours as a night sister at Stapleton Park,
Pontefract and Darrington Auxiliary Military Hospital,
Pontefract from 31 August 1915 to 4 November 1918.

70. Miss Sybil Grace Leatham, Hemsworth Hall, Wakefield.
    Age when engaged: 36. Served as a nurse at Bulford
    Military Hospital, Wiltshire from 9 August 1916 to
    11 October 1916 then Tidworth Military Hospital,
    Wiltshire from 17 October 1916 to 9 March 1917. Became
    commandant at Red Cross Hospital, Gillingham, Dorset
    from October 1917 to March 1919. 'Mentioned' on 10
    February 1919 and gained three service bars.
71. Miss Annie Littlewood, Pinderfields Road, Wakefield.
    Served 2,798 hours as a nursing sister at St John's from
    17 December 1910 (joined VAD) to 28 February 1919.
    Mentioned in Honours List, October 1917.
72. Miss Sarah Livingstone, Highfield, Sandal, Wakefield.
    Served 2,000 hours of nursing duties at Park Lane, from
    13 May 1918.
73. Mrs E. Lloyd, Westgarth Altofts, Normanton.
    Served 1,260 hours of nursing duties at St John's from
    10 August 1914, plus a year in France to October 1915.
74. Mrs Beatrice Loft, 33 Jacobs Well Lane, Wakefield.
    Served 1,500 hours of nursing duties at Park Lane from
    20 May 1918.
75. Miss Beatrice Marshall, Silcoates, Wakefield.
    Served 268 hours as a nursing sister at St John's from
    26 November 1911 to 28 February 1919.
76. Miss Mabel Martin, Snow Hill View, Wakefield.
    Served 336 hours as a nursing sister from 9 October 1913
    (joined VAD) to 28 February 1919 at St John's.
77. Miss Mabel Ethel Maughan, 119 Holmhill Place,
    Wakefield.
    Age when engaged: 36. Served as a nursing sister from
    16 November 1915 to 28 April 1916 at St A B Hospital,
    Naples with TN.
    Awarded 1915 Star.
78. Mrs Sarah Purdy McDougall (née Shepherd on Ramsey
    Isle of Man), Omar Lodge, Dewsbury Rd, Wakefield.
    Age when engaged: 29. Served as a nurse from 24
    June 1915, posted to 1st Western General Hospital in
    Fazakerley, Liverpool from 13 October 1915 and to
    France from 24 July 1918 to 23 January 1919.

Her character and work were described as exceptionally good and she was commended on 20 October 1917.

79. Miss Eva Mellard, 10 Westerman Street, Sandal Cross Lane, Wakefield.
Age when engaged: 21. Served as a nurse from 28 March 1917 to 1919 at the 2nd Northern General Hospital in Leeds.

80. Miss Jane Milner, 211 Alexandra Terrace Dewsbury Rd, Wakefield.
Served 225 hours of nursing duties from July 1918 to 1919 at Park Lane.

81. Mrs Evelyn Milsom (née Albrighton in 1891), 1 East View, High Green Rd, Altofts, Normanton.
Served as a full-time nurse from 10 June 1915 to July 1918, paid £20 a year. Wellington Hospital 10 June 1915 to 7 January 1916, Wentworth House Wakefield June 1916 to 1 January 1917, East Leeds War Hospital September 1916 to 19 April 1917, Park Lane Military Hospital, Wakefield January 1918 to July 1918.
Awarded 2 service stripes.

82. Mrs Caroline Ada Moorhouse, Pinderfields House, Wakefield.
Served 1,984 hours as a junior masseuse at St John's from 24 April 1917 to 28 February 1919.

83. Miss Marjorie Moorhouse, Springfield, Flanshaw, Wakefield.
Served full-time as GSM in charge of pantry at White Rose Auxiliary Military Hospital, Wakefield from 10 July 1918 to 1919.

84. Miss Elizabeth Nettleton, 125 High Street, Normanton.
Served for 6,394 hours as part-time a nursing sister at St John's from 6 December 1915 to 28 February 1919.

85. Miss Nellie Nettleton, Grange Street, Wakefield.
Served as GSM, 180 hours pantry work at White Rose Auxiliary Military Hospital, Wakefield, from July 1918 to 1919.

86. Mrs Gladys Palmer, Baker Street, Belle Vue, Wakefield.
Served 39 hours of nursing duties at Park Lane from 30 May 1918 to 1919.

87. Miss Laura Perkins, 24 Howard Street Wakefield.
    Served 6,663 hours as a nursing sister at St John's from
    1 August 1915 to 28 February 1919.
88. Miss Phyllis Pilkington, Chevet Park, Wakefield.
    Served 8,290 hours as a nursing sister at St John's from
    14 August 1914 to 28 February 1919.
89. Miss Marguerite C. Purton, Heath House, Pinderfields Rd,
    Wakefield.
    Served 1,580 hours as a nursing sister at St John's from
    12 June 1918 to 28 February 1919.
90. Miss Elizabeth Ethel Rhodes, 7 South Parade Wakefield.
    Served as GSM, pantry work at White Rose Auxiliary
    Military Hospital, Wakefield, from 14 July 1918 to 1919.
91. Mrs Emily Jane Richardson, Wyvenhoe, Westfield Rd,
    Wakefield.
    Served 484 hours as a nursing sister at St John's from
    3 February 1917 to 28 February 1919.
92. Mrs Alice Roberts, 1 Hague Terrace, Hemsworth,
    Wakefield.
    Served as a full-time nurse at Stapleton Park Auxiliary
    Hospital, Pontefract, from 16 February 1917 to 26 June
    1917.
93. Mrs Marion Anderson Saville, Calder Grove, Wakefield.
    Served for about twelve months on sewing duties.
94. Miss Margaret Scarlett, Beech House, St Johns,
    Wakefield.
    Served 4,088 hours as a nursing sister at St John's from
    2 February 1918 to 28 February 1919.
95. Miss Evelyn Gwendoline Seeley, Clarendon Street,
    Wakefield.
    Served 2,688 hours of nursing duties at St John's from
    1 August 1915 to 28 February. 1919.
96. Miss Emily Smith, 24 High Street, Normanton.
    Served 1,188 hours as a nursing sister at St John's from
    7 February 1917 to 28 February 1919.
97. Miss Sarah Speight, 24 Grantley St, Warrengate,
    Wakefield.
    Served as full-time nurse, mainly night duty at Park Lane
    from 30 May 1918 to 1919.

98. Miss May Stenton, West Street, Ossett Rd, Wakefield
Served 2,500 hours as part-time nurse at Park Lane from
1 September 1917 to 1919.

99. Miss Margaret Stonehouse, South Parade, Wakefield.
Served 420 hours of recreation room duties at St John's
from 19 May 1917 to 28 February 1919.

100. Miss Norah Catherine Stringer, 38 Bond Street,
Wakefield.
Served 3,590 hours as a nursing sister at St John's from
27 June 1918 to 28 February 1919.

101. Miss Mabel Sutcliffe, Regent St, Belle Vue, Wakefield.
Served 304 hours as a nursing sister at St John's from
12 January 1911 (joined VAD) to 28 February 1919.

102. Miss Emily May Sutton, 65 Pinderfields Road, Wakefield.
Age when engaged: 24. Served as a nurse at West
Bridgford Military Hospital, Nottinghamshire, paid £20
a year, from 22 December 1917 to 8 May 1919.
Awarded 1 scarlet stripe for efficiency, 14 February 1919.

103. Miss Mary Swann, 25 Hatfeild Street, Wakefield.
Served as full-time nurse at Park Lane from March to
September 1918.

104. Mrs Mildred Taylor, Hemsworth Lane Ends, Wakefield.
Served 2,310 hours as a trained nurse, sister-in-charge
at Darrington Auxiliary Military Hospital, Pontefract
and Stapleton Park, Pontefract, from 29 May 1917 to
11 February 1918.

105. Miss Frances Elizabeth Percy Tew, Heath, Wakefield.
Served 8,080 hours as a nursing sister at St John's from
14 August 1914 to 28 February 1919.

106. Miss Adele Thomason, 4 Garden Row, Crofton,
Wakefield.
Served as a senior housemaid in nurses' hostel at 2nd
Northern General Hospital Beckett's Park, Leeds, at
£20 a year, from 25 May 1915 and was still serving on
24 April 1919.

107. Mrs Jane Thomason, 4 Garden Row, Crofton, Wakefield.
Served as a senior cook in nurses' hostel at 2nd Northern
General Hospital Beckett's Park, Leeds, at £35 a year,
from 12 April 1917 and was still serving on 28 April 1919.

108. Miss Irene Townend, 8, Love Lane, Wakefield.
Age when engaged: 21. Served as a nurse at Military
Hospital, Ripon from 13 February 1917 to 30 April 1919.
109. Miss Beatrice Varley, Knoll View, East Ardsley, Wakefield
Age when engaged: 21. Served as a nurse at Napsbury
Military Hospital, St Albans from 20 July 1917 to 20
March 1918.
Awarded scarlet efficiency strip on 20 March 1918.
110. Miss Maud Wainwright, 11 Bernels St, Wakefield.
Served 180 hours as part-time nurse at St John's from
October 1918 to February 1919.
111. Miss Annie Walker, 18 Regent Street, Belle Vue,
Wakefield.
Age when engaged: 32. Served as full-time nurse at East
Leeds Military Hospital, paid £20 a year, from June 1916
to March 1918.
Awarded service bar.
112. Miss Ethel W. Walker, Boyne Hill House, Chapelthorpe,
Wakefield.
Served 2,688 hours as a nursing sister at St John's from
5 November 1914 to 28 February 1919.
113. Miss Margaret Irene Walker, Boyne Hill House,
Chapelthorpe, Wakefield.
Age when engaged: 27. Served 8,520 hours as a a nursing
sister at No. 8 General Hospital, Rouen, France from 26
October 1915 to 26 November 1916, Cambridge Hospital,
Aldershot from 23 February 1917 to 24 April 1917 and at
St John's until 28 February 1919.
114. Miss (Nellie) Walsh, 126 Northgate Wakefield.
Served 726 hours as part-time a nursing sister at St from
17 December 1910 (joined VAD) to 28 February 1919.
115. Miss Noel Wentworth, Woolley Park Nr. Wakefield.
Served 4,148 hours as a nursing sister at St John's from
2 February 1918 to 28 February 1919.
116. Mrs Elizabeth Selman Wilkins, 44 College Grove Road
Wakefield.
Served 2,000 hours of nursing duties at Park Lane from
30 May 1918 to April 1919.

117. Miss Sarah Eliza Wilkinson, c/o Mr Eggleston, Cross
Square, Wakefield.
Served 160 hours as nurse at Park Lane from July to
October 1918.

118. Miss Dorothy Williams, Bleak House, Sandal, Wakefield.
Served as a full-time nurse at Park Lane from October
1917 to October 1918.

119. Miss Jessie Williamson, School House, East Ardsley.
Served 9,238 hours as a nursing sister at St John's from
11 July 1917 to 28 February 1919.

120. Miss Louisa Wilson, Stanley Road, Wakefield.
Served 2,688 hours as a nursing sister at St John's from
12 September 1913 (joined VAD) to 28 February 1919.

121. Mrs Winn, Walton Hall, Wakefield.
Served 264 hours at Stapleton Park, Pontefract from
23 June 1915 to 21 August 1915.

122. Miss Annie Wormald, York Street, Wakefield.
Served 1,090 hours as a nursing sister at St John's from
26 February 1913 (joined VAD) to 28 February 1919.

123. Miss Laura Annie Wright, 41 Queen Street, Wakefield.
Age when engaged: 33. Served as a nurse, at £20 a year,
at 3rd London General Military Hospital, Wandsworth
from 21 June 1915 to 10 September 1916, transferred to
Infarta Military Hospital, Malta to 3 December 1917,
then returned to Wandsworth to April 1919.

124. Miss Susan Mary Wright, The Folly, Outwood, Wakefield.
Served more than 2,688 hours as a nursing sister, first
for eight months as a probationer in London and
Birmingham hospitals, then at St John's from January
1918 to February 1919.

Babies Welcome Team on Mental and Child Welfare Subcommittee 1930

1. **Mrs Elizabeth May Matilda Appleyard**, (née Abbey) 20 Belgravia Road. DOB 13 May 1890 (Husband Wilfred H. Appleyard, certified colliery surveyor, married 1916).

2. **Mrs Gertrude Jane Butler**, (née Burnley) 11, Henry Street. DOB 3 June 1887 (husband John Thomas Butler, railway goods guard, married 1906).

3. **Mrs Ivy Cudworth**, (née Bentley) 8, School Rd, Lupset. DOB 20 November 1902 (husband Charles W. Cudworth, railway goods guard, married 1919).

4. **Mrs Annie Hudson**, (née Gledhill) College Grove House. DOB 2 October 1866 (widow of Albert Hudson, auctioneer/corn merchant, married 1891).

5. **Mrs Alice Ann Martin**, (née Rollinson) 16, Wentworth Street. DOB 1 May 1872 (husband David Frederick Martin, wholesale smallwares dealer, married 1902). Mother of Edith Mary Martin the typing teacher at the Technical College.

6. **Miss Edith Gladys Sutcliffe**, 188, Doncaster Road. DOB 18 April 1895 at Almondbury.

7. **Mrs Hannah Caroline Wrigglesworth**, (née Brown in Wigan.) 5, Westfield View. DOB 4 August 1878 (husband Walter Wrigglesworth retired male asylum nurse, married 1906).

Wakefield's Healthcare Staff

Health Visitor Staff, 1921

- **Sarah S. Thorp:** Certificate of Royal Sanitary Institute for

  i.   Inspector of nuisances

  ii. Maternity & child welfare

  iii. Health visitors & school nurses

  Plus Central Midwives Board certificate (CMB)
  Offices held: Health Visitor, superintendent of Market St Child Welfare Centre (CWC), School Nurse and TB nurse

- **Edith Greenwood:** Trained nurse and CMB Certificate. Offices as above, but superintendent for Thornes Lane CWC
- **Ada Knox:** as above, superintendent for Belle Vue CWC
- **Ellen R. Paver:** as above, superintendent for Homestead and Alverthorpe CWCs
- **Eliza E. Bell:** as above, superintendent for Eastmoor CWC

- **A.J. Peck:** Trained Nurse, matron at Fever Hospital
- **H.J. More:** Trained Nurse and CMB certificate, matron at Maternity Hospital

Wakefield City Maternity Hospital Staff, 1939

Dr Jessie Eeles	Medical practitioner	DOB	6 September 1899
Kate Perkins	Matron	DOB	5 May 1898
Amy Clayton	Deputy Matron	DOB	30 May 1899
Ann Pitts	Night Sister	DOB	5 July 1888
Agnes Cameron	Nurse	DOB	1 December 1907
Elizabeth McWhirter	Day Sister	DOB	12 March 1907
Mary Blacker	Day Sister	DOB	9 January 1913
Minnie Melville	Staff Midwife	DOB	26 January 1915
Agnes Steedmaster	Staff Midwife	DOB	20 October 1905
Violet Deepnose	Midwife	DOB	31 May 1907
Ruth Senior	Midwife	DOB	27 December 1905
Constance Caldwell	Midwife	DOB	13 July 1905
Doris K. Evans	Midwife	DOB	22 April 1903

Bibliography

Clarkson, Henry, *Memories of Merrie Wakefield* (W.H.Milnes, 1889)

Dawson, Paul L., *Secret Wakefield* (Amberley, 2015)

Ellis, Norman, *Bygone Wakefield and District Volume* 2 (M&D Rigg publications, 1992)

Hardcastle, Margaret, *Wakefield Girls High School* 1878-1978 (WGSF, 1978)

Petyt, Angela, *Victorian & Edwardian Wakefield* (1999-2000) All rights reserved

Taylor, Kate (and others), *Aspects of Wakefield Volume 2* (Wharncliffe Books, 1999)

Taylor, Kate (and others), *Aspects of Wakefield Volume 3* (Wharncliffe Books, 2001)

Taylor, Kate, *Worthies of Wakefield* (Wakefield Historical Society, 2004)

Taylor, Kate, *Not so Merry Wakefield* (Wharncliffe Books, 2005)

Taylor, Kate, *The Making of Wakefield 1801-1900* (Wharncliffe Books, 2008)

Various, *More Memories of Wakefield* (True North Books, 1999)

Wakefield District Committee for European Architectural Heritage Year, *Wakefield District Heritage* (Wakefield Express, 1976)

Walker, Charlie, *Wakefield, Its Times and its Peoples through 1930-60* (Walker, 2001)

Resources

West Yorkshire Archive Service

- Documents relating to the Industrial home for discharged female prisoners (also known as St John's Community Home/ West Riding Institutional Home for women)
- Register of Wakefield Reformatory School 1856–65
- Wakefield Business and Professional Women's Club minutes 1944–50
- House of Recovery Documents
- Wakefield City Police: A Brief History of the Wakefield City Police
- From Wakefield Constabulary 1848–1968 by Colin Jackson
- Wakefield Mothers' Union minutes 1895–1917
- Co-operative Women's Guild minutes 1908–17

Wakefield Local Studies Library

- Wakefield Council meeting minutes 1906–1950
- Various others

Ancestry
- *William White's Directory of 1854*
- *Slater's Commercial Directory of 1855*, (Durham, Northumberland, and Yorkshire Royal National Commercial Directory, 1855, Slaters Royal National Commercial Directory of the Northern Counties, Vol 1) (Ancestry)
- Census records
- Births, Marriage and Death Records
- Burdett's Nursing Registers

Find My Past

- 1939 Register

The British Newspaper Archive

Red Cross First World War nursing records: https://vad.redcross.org.uk

Histpop.org (Online Historical Population Reports)

Grace's Guide to British Industrial History: http://www.gracesguide.co.uk/

Children's Homes: http://www.childrenshomes.org.uk

'Twixt Aire and Calder: http://www.twixtaireandcalder.org.uk

Wakefield Family History Sharing: http://www.wakefieldfhs.org.uk/

Index

Municipal Maternity
Hospital, 101
Refuge and Reformation
School
see St John's Home for
Girls, House of Refuge
Sanitary Aid Society, 92, 95
School Board, 15, 17, 68
School of Art, 15, 28–9,
31, 34
Soroptomists' Club, 144
Technical College, 32–3
Victoria District Nursing
Association, 108
Women's Conservative
Association, 143–6
Women's Relief, 138
Women's Suffrage Society,
130–7
Yards, 92, 110
Walker, Ann, 6
Walker, Miss Annie, 180
Walker, Miss Ethel W., 180
Walker, Miss Margaret
Irene, 180
Walley, Miss N., 132
See also Wakefield Women's
Suffrage Society
Walsh, Miss Nellie, 180
Walshaw, Miss June, 167
Walton Hall Maternity
Hospital, 103
Walton, Miss Molly, 167
Walton, Sarah Ann, 164
Ward, Ellen, 163
Warrington, Mrs A.I., 167
Wartime nurseries, 59

Watmough, Mrs Agnes
Florence, 132
See also Wakefield
Women's Suffrage
Society
Weldon, Miss R., 70
Wentworth House Military
Hospital, 67, 170
Wentworth, Miss Noel, 180
Wesleyan Training School,
5, 12
West Riding
Agricultural Committee, 51
Pauper Lunatic Asylum, 4
Proprietary School, 5, 10
West Riding Industrial
Home for Discharged
Female Prisoners
see House of Refuge, St
John's Home for Girls
Westerman Mary, 6
Westle, Miss A., 167
Whitaker, Ann, 164
Whitefield, Mary, 4
Whiteley, Elizabeth, 163
Whitfield, Mary A., 162
Wilby, Mary Alice, 164
Wilde, Mrs Amelia, 166
Wilkins, Mrs Elizabeth
Selman, 180
Wilkinson, Audrey, 56
see also Women's Land
Army
Wilkinson, Miss, 18
Wilkinson, Miss Emily, 19
Wilkinson, Miss Sarah
Eliza, 181